Helen Rhiannon

Helen Rhiannon is an award-winning designer specializing in bespoke wedding dresses. Helen was fortunate to grow up by the picturesque coastline of Gower in Swansea, Wales, where she still lives. She creates beautiful, timeless, handmade gowns from her studio.

Helen has gained a solid reputation for her superlative dressmaking skills which has led her to share her knowledge and passion through teaching. Helen set up the 'All Sewn Up Wales' sewing workshops in 2010, designed to help people learn and develop new skills, whilst meeting like-minded creative people. Her expert tuition has attracted students from around the world and she regularly makes guest appearances on national television.

For more information on Helen's work, visit www.allsewnupwales.co.uk where you can also find an extensive online sewing shop, a wide range of tutorials and Helen's YouTube channel.

DRESSMAKING
THE EASY GUIDE

DRESSMAKING
THE EASY GUIDE

HELEN RHIANNON

SEARCH PRESS

Dedication and acknowledgements

I would like to say a huge thank you to Katie French and Search Press for believing in my idea and allowing me to create my dream book. Thank you, Becky, for starting the journey and Beth, who took over as editor and has been incredibly patient, helpful and a pure delight throughout.

Thank you, Mark, for being the perfect photographer to capture every step of this book. Thank you, Maz, for allowing me to manage a photoshoot in my beautiful hometown with the fabulous Leanna, Kelly and 'When Charlie Met Hannah' Dream Team!
Thank you to my awesome Pattern Tester Fairies.

I'd also like to thank my family for their endless love and support throughout this journey. I love you all. Mum, thanks for passing on the love of sewing.

And lastly, a special thank you to the incredible NHS in Swansea, Cardiff and Bristol for everything they do for our Heart Warrior, Morgan, my little superhero.

The projects in this book have been made using metric measurements, and the imperial equivalents provided have been calculated following standard conversion practices. The imperial measurements are often rounded to the nearest ⅛in for ease of use except in rare circumstances; however, if you need more exact measurements, there are a number of excellent online converters that you can use. Always use either metric or imperial measurements, not a combination of both.

First published in 2023

Search Press Limited
Wellwood, North Farm Road,
Tunbridge Wells, Kent TN2 3DR

Text copyright © Helen Rhiannon, 2023.

Photographs by Mark Davison for Search Press Studios, Ltd; except for pages 1, 3 (centre) 5, 7 (top), 8 (right), 13, 39, 43, 47, 73, 81, 87, 91, 120, 135 and 143 by When Charlie Met Hannah; and pages 7 (bottom) and 46 by Little Things Photography; photograph on page 146 (top centre) by Helen Rhiannon.

Photographs and design copyright © Search Press Ltd. 2023

ISBN: 978-1-78221-891-3
ebook ISBN: 978-1-78126-887-2
Pattern sheet ISBN: 978-1-80092-215-0

Suppliers

If you have difficulty in obtaining any of the materials and equipment mentioned in this book, then please visit the Search Press website for details of suppliers:
www.searchpress.com

Extra information on setting up your sewing machine for dressmaking can be downloaded free from the Bookmarked Hub: www.bookmarkedhub.com. Search for this book by title or ISBN: the files can be found under 'Book Extras'. Membership of the Bookmarked online community is free.

Additional copies of the dressmaking patterns are available for purchase from the Search Press website.

Find Helen:

- At her website: www.allsewnupwales.co.uk
- At sewing workshops: All Sewn Up Wales
- On Facebook: www.facebook.com/AllSewnUpWales
- On Instagram: @all_sewn_up_wales

Publishers' note

All the step-by-step photographs in this book feature the author, Helen Rhiannon, demonstrating dressmaking. No models have been used.

CONTENTS

Introduction   6
Tools   10
Your sewing machine   14
Sewing know-how   18
Fabrics   24
Sewing language   32

GETTING STARTED

1. Sizing   40
2. Pattern cutting   48
3. Adjusting your blocks   52
4. Making your sample   60
5. Altering your sample   74

MAKING THE DRESS YOUR OWN

6. Adapting the pattern   92
   - necklines   92
   - sleeves   104
   - skirts   122
   - collars   136
   - pockets   139
7. Finishing your dress   142
   - constructing your garment   142
   - zip closures   146
8. Separates   154
   - tops   154
   - skirts: adding a waistband or facing   156
9. Taking it further   159

Index   160

introduction

Welcome to *Dressmaking: the easy guide!*

My name is Helen Rhiannon and I love creating my own unique dresses to wear! In this book, I will teach you how to measure yourself, how to understand and adapt a pattern, and how to cut out and sew your own bespoke dresses from scratch. You will choose the neckline, sleeves and skirt shape, and adjust each dress to fit your own unique shape. The result will be your own personalized wardrobe, bursting with stylish clothes that fit and flatter your body. And trust me, there's nothing quite like the first time someone asks you, 'where did you get your dress from?'... and you can happily tell them that you made it – followed by the proclamation that 'it has pockets!'.

This is, as the title suggests, an easy guide to making your own dresses. I am starting from scratch and keeping the language easy to follow for any skill level. I have run sewing workshops since 2010 and have spent hours teaching people to make garments.

First, I'll run through the simple techniques you'll need and give some suggestions for tools and materials (see pages 10–31). Next, I'll explain how the patterns work and what the terminology means, as it can seem like another language (pages 32–39), and I'll talk about sizing and how to choose the correct size, as this is key to creating a successful and flattering garment (pages 40–47).

You will learn how to make a sample garment, or toile, to help you perfect the fit of your dress based on your own measurements (pages 60–73), and on pages 74–91 I will show you how to adjust your sample so that it fits you perfectly.

Then, on pages 92–159, I have broken down the elements of a dress so that you can mix and match your favourite styles to create your own unique, well-fitted wardrobe. You can choose different necklines, sleeves and skirt shapes to help you sew a range of personalized and flattering garments.

Who is this book for?

This book will teach you how to make and fit a beautiful dress for yourself – whatever shape and size you are. Most of us have trouble shopping for well-fitting clothes. The same applies to making clothes from a pattern. Only a handful of people can cut the size stated and have the garment fit perfectly. It doesn't help that patterns are given in UK, EU and American sizes to confuse everyone. I am 1.8m (5ft 11in) tall and have hips and curves, so finding clothes that fit and flatter is very difficult. The waistlines never sit on my waist, and everything is always too short on the body and in length. I also enjoy wearing clothes that are bright and colourful and not necessarily what is on trend. I only buy and make clothes that fit me well, and that I will keep in my wardrobe for years to come.

This book caters for all shapes and sizes. I was lucky to have a group of ladies who tried and tested the patterns and then made their own unique dresses to fit them. You can see a shot of them all looking stunning in their amazing creations below.

To make things less daunting, I have created a bespoke numerical size chart with sizes ranging from 1 to 19. You simply choose the size number based on your measurements. Once you choose your correct size, I will guide you through how you get that perfect fit, whether you are tall or short, curvy or slim, and have lumps and bumps in various places! We come in so many different shapes and sizes, and that is what makes women so unique and fabulous, so why not make your clothes unique and fabulous too?

My pattern-testing fairies, who are proudly modelling the dresses they have made based on the patterns in this book.

How to use this book

To start your dressmaking journey, you will begin by measuring yourself against the bespoke size chart on page 45 and then selecting the closest measurements to yours. You will then trace off the appropriate size pattern blocks to work from.

You can make some minor alterations to the blocks before cutting out and making a sample (toile). You then alter your sample and transfer those alterations to your patterns.

The next step is choosing what neckline, sleeve and skirt designs you want to create to complete your finished dress.

The beauty of this book is that you can create over 80 different looks, just by mixing and matching the key elements of a dress. Once you perfect the fit, you can then choose from **four different necklines**, **four different sleeves** and **five different skirt ideas**. You can also learn how to add a **collar** and **pockets** to transform your outfit!

From paper pattern...

Starting with your paper patterns, such as the Front Bodice pattern piece shown, alterations are made to the paper pattern before it is cut out in calico (see pages 52–59).

...to calico sample, or toile...

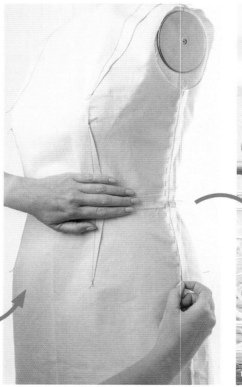

A sample in calico is made to allow you to perfect the fit (see pages 60–91). The sample (toile) also allows you to consider which neckline, sleeve and skirt you might like to try (see pages 92–135).

...to finished, customized outfit!

This finished dress is one of many combinations of dresses, tops and skirts you can make by combining different features (see pages 92–159).

Necklines

Curved neckline
See page 94

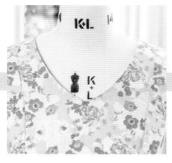

'V' neckline
See page 95

Sweetheart neckline
See page 96

Boatneck neckline
See page 97

Sleeves

Flared sleeve
See page 108

Capped sleeve
See page 110

Puff sleeve
See page 113

Butterfly sleeve
See page 116

Skirts

Fitted skirt
See page 122

Gathered skirt
See page 126

Circle skirt
See page 128

A-line skirt
See page 130

Box-pleated skirt
See page 132

Additions

Collars
See page 136

Pockets
See page 139

tools

You don't need to buy every tool available to be a skilful dressmaker. I am fairly traditional myself and have a small selection of must-haves, which I will share with you.

Anything else you can gather is a bonus – optional extras are shown on page 12.

My must-have list

1. Sewing machine   A machine from a reputable brand will last you years – more on this on pages 14–15.

2. Tape measure   For measuring the body and the patterns. Make sure it includes both centimetres and inches.

3. Paper scissors   A good sharp pair of scissors for cutting out your paper patterns.

4. Click pencil   To get an accurate line when drawing patterns, use a click pencil (mechanical pencil) or a normal pencil with a sharpened point.

5. Masking tape or brown paper tape   Use this for making alterations to your patterns. You can write on it and tear it easily.

6. Red pen   For pattern markings (grainlines).

7. Pattern master   This is a special technical ruler, which is a must-have when drafting or altering patterns. Use it to draw accurate straight and curved lines, add seam allowances and mark grainlines.

8. Pattern paper   Use plain pattern paper or dot-and-cross paper, which helps with accuracy. Make sure the paper isn't too thick as you need to be able to trace through it. Investing in long lengths of wide paper will save you having to stick smaller pieces of paper together.

9. Dressmaking scissors   Good-quality dressmaking scissors with a sharp tip are essential. Quality scissors are not cheap but buy them once and they will last. You can get them sharpened by a professional.

10. Unpicker   Unfortunately, you will need one of these however expert you are! Use these to unpick stitching when mistakes are made by sliding the sharp point under each stitch and cutting, using the blade.

11. Good-quality dressmaking pins   Do not scrimp on pins. They ideally need to be long and narrow. Glass-head pins are fine as they are easy to pick up. I personally buy nickel-plated pins, which are 34mm × 0.6mm.

12. Iron   A good, clean iron is needed for all parts of garment construction. A non-drip model is essential, as drips can leave watermarks on some fabrics. I use a spare iron for ironing on interfacing, to keep the main iron as clean as possible. (See block fusing on page 100.) I keep the temperature setting at medium (2 dots).

13. Small embroidery scissors   It's always a good idea to keep a small, sharp pair of embroidery scissors handy for trimming certain edges and threads, among other things.

14. Tailors' chalk/chalk pencils   Tailors' chalk is a great tool for marking features on fabric and can be rubbed off or blotted off with water. There are also several fabric pens on the market which allow you to draw thinner lines onto fabric and they come off over time, with the application of water or sometimes heat. Always test chalk and pens on a scrap of fabric.

15. Hand-sewing needles   A selection of hand-sewing needles is always useful for finishing off thread ends or sewing on buttons and trims.

16. Interfacing (not shown)   Interfacing is a fabric that is applied to facings to stiffen the fabric for a firmer finish and helps prevent necklines and armholes from stretching. It comes in white, grey and black. I prefer to use mediumweight, iron-on interfacing but you can get a range of thicknesses and types.

OPTIONAL EXTRAS

1. Cutting mat and rotary cutter   I have several A1 (84.1 × 59.4cm / 33⅛ × 23⅜in) mats on my cutting table permanently, as this allows me to lay fabric on the table and cut it out with a rotary cutter. The mats are self-healing, which means you can use them for a long time before they start wearing.

Personally, I find using a rotary cutter more accurate than scissors when cutting out a garment, as you can get nice and close to the pattern edge for accuracy. It is easier on your hands than using scissors all of the time and you can also layer up your fabric and cut through a few layers in one go, which saves time and effort. It also means that your fabric will not move or stretch once it is pinned or weighted down as you are not lifting it like you would when cutting with scissors. Make sure no pins are under your fabric as this will blunt your blade.

Using a rotary cutter does take a bit of practice when trying it for the first time so practise on scraps. I do still use scissors when cutting as they are needed to get into tight corners and for certain pattern markings.

2. Overlocker (serger) (not shown)   An overlocker (serger) is a different machine from a sewing machine. It gives a professional finish to the seam edges as it cuts and finishes your seam allowances, which eliminates fraying when your garment is worn and when washed.

Overlockers can be hard to thread, although more upmarket models thread themselves. You can always learn to thread one at a local class or online. Once you use one it is hard to go back! Do not worry if you don't have an overlocker, however, as you can use a zigzag stitch to neaten your seam edges (see page 22).

3. Concealed zipper foot   A normal zipper foot comes with all sewing machines but you will need a concealed zipper foot if you want to put concealed zips into your garments as these give a beautifully neat and discreet finish to a garment (see pages 146–153).

4. Walking foot   This can be handy when sewing layers that can slip or that are quite thick. I personally prefer to use a normal foot for dressmaking, but some people swear by them for all forms of sewing.

5. Tracing wheel   This handy contraption allows you to trace a pattern easily onto paper. Its serrated edge leaves holes in the paper so you can then join the dots on your copy.

6. Sleeve ironing board (not shown)   For those tricky tasks, such as ironing the sleeve seam as this is difficult to do on a standard board without creating unwanted creases. An ironing ham is also useful when ironing anything with curves, such as bust seams.

How to make this dress
This casual yet stylish dress features puff sleeves (see page 113), a gathered skirt (page 126) and a curved neckline (page 94).
I made it here in a printed cotton fabric for a relaxed daywear look, but you could create a very different dress by using a lightweight wool fabric to transform it into a sophisticated winter staple dress.

your sewing machine

A sewing machine is a crucial tool for your sewing adventures. Your sewing machine will become your best friend as you start to make your own wardrobe.

> Do your research and get a quality machine which will last for years to come.

When sewing your own wardrobe, the right sewing machine will make life easier and your sewing experience much more enjoyable.

I bought my first sewing machine, a Janome, when I was 16 and taking a school exam in Textiles. It is quite basic with only a handful of extra stitches. I have had it serviced a number of times over the years by my trusted local sewing-machine shop (thank you, Mike and Tony at Cliffords, Swansea!). My machine is now over 25 years old (yes, I am showing my age!) but *everything* I have ever made has been sewn on that machine. This includes hundreds of household items, clothing, toys, and a ridiculous amount of occasion-wear and bridal-wear. I mean it when I say, do your research and get a quality machine that will last for years to come.

Choosing a sewing machine

I'm not going to tell you to spend a small fortune on a sewing machine, but I do have some advice for you.

◆ Get a good-quality brand!

Do your research and, if possible, **visit a local shop** so you can talk through your needs. You can even attend a local sewing class where you can use their machines and see what you like. I offer this service at my sewing workshops, and people find it easier to buy a machine once they know how to use it. You could consider buying a second-hand machine to save on cost but again, do your research.

If you are serious about dressmaking and sewing in general, you will appreciate a good-quality machine which will last. You do not have to break the bank but if you buy cheap, you are more likely to buy twice.

Servicing a machine can cost quite a lot of money, so bear that in mind. Good-quality branded machines can be fixed, unlike their cheaper counterparts. You can also buy a whole host of useful attachments for branded machines, such as a concealed zipper foot.

◆ Consider your options

Every sewing machine will have a few different length straight stitches, a few zigzag settings and most likely a buttonhole function. These **settings** will be all you need when you first start dressmaking. The cost goes up if the machine has features and additional stitches that make it easier to use. Modern digital machines are more expensive but they are foolproof and make adding details such as buttonholes very simple!

You will also want to consider one of two **bobbin options**: a drop-in bobbin or a front-loading bobbin. A drop-in bobbin is easy, and quite stress-free, to load: the bobbin is dropped into the machine and you are ready to sew. This feature is found on most modern machines. A front-loading bobbin is inserted into a bobbin holder before being put into the machine. This must be done correctly for the machine to work. This type of bobbin is found on industrial machines and some cheaper domestic machines. Once you know how to load a bobbin, it will become second nature.

◆ Check the guarantee

Buying from a recommended retailer means your machine will come with a warranty/guarantee, which means you can get it repaired or replaced if anything goes wrong.

Setting up your sewing machine

Being able to set up your machine correctly plays a huge part
in making clothing successfully. Here are some useful tips:

NEEDLES

• Buy only good-quality sewing-machine needles by brands
  such as Schmetz or Janome. Cheap needles can ruin your
  machine so don't take the risk.

• Use the correct needle size for your project. I use a size 12
  when making my dresses in cotton. I change to a size 14 or 16
  when sewing denim.

• Use a new needle at the start of every new project.

• If you hear a thumping sound when sewing, check that
  your needle isn't blunt as it may be struggling to pierce
  the fabric. Also, check that your needle isn't snagging your
  fabric when sewing as this is another sign of a blunt needle.
  If in doubt, change your needle to a new one when starting
  a new garment.

• Dispose of needles safely – do not throw them directly into
  the bin. Have a box handy by your machine, drop your used
  needles inside, seal the box when full and then discard it
  responsibly to prevent injury to others.

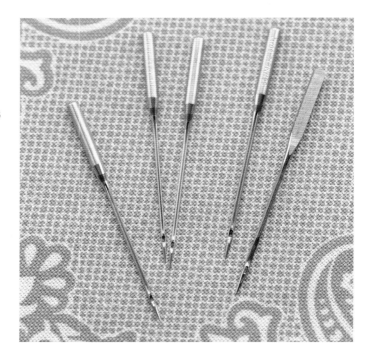

Which needle should I use?

Sewing-machine needles are sized in metric and imperial. The smaller the numbers
the finer the needle. You can buy special needles for: stretch, jersey, jeans, leather,
quilting, embroidery and topstitch. Here is a handy chart for which needles to use, for
each type of woven fabric:

Needle size	Fabric type
60/8	Silks, sheer fabrics and organza
65/9	
70/10	Cotton lawn and lining fabrics
75/11	
80/12	Cotton
90/14	Linen, light denims and cushion fabrics
100/16	Denim
110/18	Upholstery fabrics, leather, vinyls and PVC
120/20	Thick denim, thick leather and heavy canvas

THREADS

I use brands such as Coats or Gütermann: Coats Moon Threads are excellent value for money and can be used on an overlocker (serger) as well as a sewing machine.

When matching the thread to your fabric, unravel some thread and lay it directly onto the fabric to help match the colour. Always keep matching thread on your bobbin for a neat finish.

Thread tension

Correct thread tension on a row of stitching is when the top thread and bobbin thread look exactly the same on both sides of your fabric, meaning that they are perfectly balanced. There should be no loops or irregularities.

On most domestic sewing machines, the thread tension dial is set to 4. (Always check your machine manual.) My personal rule is 'put the tension on 4 and don't change it unless you know why you are changing it!' I rarely change my tension and I sew all types of fabrics from cottons to silks.

Handy tip if attending a class

- Ask to film the teacher setting up your machine so you can get it right when at home without that one-to-one help.

- The next best thing is to search for a video of your exact machine online as you will hopefully find a tutorial to watch on your machine or something very similar. I have a few videos on my website (see page 4), which may help.

Tips

- A higher number on the dial will tighten the tension. A lower number on the dial will loosen the tension. To use a particularly thick top thread, you will need to loosen the tension. Experiment on scrap fabric until you are happy with the tension.

- Practise stitching on a piece of scrap fabric before sewing your garment. If your threads are unbalanced and loops are showing, before changing your tension you should make sure your machine is threaded properly, your bobbin is wound properly and your needle is sharp.

sewing know-how

SEAM ALLOWANCE

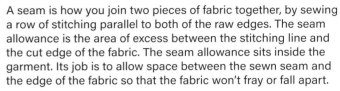

A seam is how you join two pieces of fabric together, by sewing a row of stitching parallel to both of the raw edges. The seam allowance is the area of excess between the stitching line and the cut edge of the fabric. The seam allowance sits inside the garment. Its job is to allow space between the sewn seam and the edge of the fabric so that the fabric won't fray or fall apart.

A standard seam allowance is commonly 1cm (⅜in) or a slightly more generous 1.5cm (⅝in), which allows more room to alter and finish seams. You can choose how much seam allowance you want to work with when creating your patterns (see page 36).

How to prepare and pin seams correctly

- Take the two pieces of fabric you are joining. With the **right sides of the fabric facing each other** (explained throughout as 'right sides together', or **RST**), place the raw edges together. Make sure the raw edges sit exactly in line with each other. You will sew onto the wrong side of the fabric.

- Secure the fabrics in place using pins, which will help with accuracy. Place a pin at the top of the seam and one at the bottom, matching the finished edges accurately. Then space pins evenly in between.

- Do not sew over pins! You will always run the risk of snapping your needle if it hits a pin, and small fragments of the needle can fly towards your face. Your eyes are precious! If you pin horizontally (see Tips, below), you can remove your pins just before they go under your machine foot.

- Do not remove your pins too early, as your fabric may move.

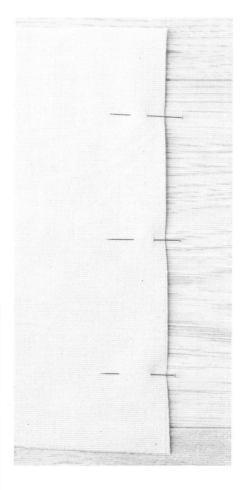

Tips
- Take time to get the positioning right and pin as much as you need to.
- Don't be afraid to over-pin.
- Always position your pins horizontally across your seam as you can sew up to the pin and remove it just before you sew that spot, keeping your garment in position throughout. If you keep the pin head on the right of the seam edge, you can easily remove it; if you are left-handed, you may prefer to keep the pin head on the left.

NEEDLE POSITIONS

You can either position your needle in the centre of the foot, or to the left, when sewing a straight line. Wherever you prefer to position the needle, just make sure that you measure the correct seam allowance from the needle to the edge of the fabric.

Every machine has slightly different guidelines alongside the foot and needle to help. If you are unsure, use a tape measure to measure from the needle to where the seam allowance should be, whether it is 1cm (⅜in) or 1.5cm (⅝in).

Showing the seam allowance at 1cm (⅜in) with the needle in the central position.

Showing the seam allowance at 1cm (⅜in) with the needle in the left position.

Tip

• You can always put a bit of masking tape or paper tape on your sewing machine to use as a guide if it doesn't have guidelines already.

GETTING READY TO SEW

When sewing garments, I recommend the stitch length to be on 2.5 and no longer.

• Always start a few millimetres in from the top edge of your fabric, otherwise the teeth may not catch your fabric to move it along.

• When you are ready to sew, lower your presser foot and make sure the edge of the fabric is along the correct guideline for your chosen seam allowance.

• Always hand-wind your needle down into the fabric to start, so you know there are no obstructions and that you are in the right position to sew.

• Never hand-wind backwards – *always* forwards.

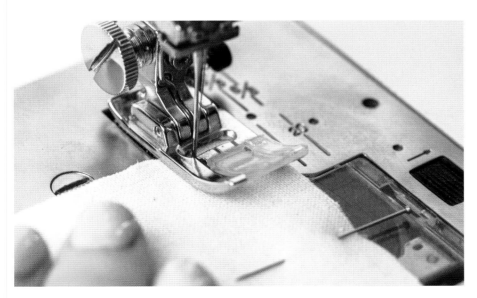

HOW TO SEW A SEAM

- Always backstitch at the start of a seam to secure the thread ends. To do this, go forward two stitches, then go back two stitches, then continue to sew the length of the seam.

- You can hold your fabric in many ways, depending on whether you are right- or left-handed. Just keep trying new ways until you feel comfortable.

- Use your fingertips to lightly guide the fabric through the machine.

- When sewing, focus on the seam edge directly in front of the foot. If you look too far ahead, you may start to pull the fabric off track. Use your fingertips to keep it steady and the edge of your fabric in line with your guide.

  - Let the machine take the fabric through at its own pace. Your job is to guide your fabric and maintain the seam allowance. You should not need to push or pull the fabric.
  - Sometimes if you are sewing something bulky, you can help your fabric through, but your machine should still be doing the hard work.
  - Try to keep your fabric flat as it goes through the machine.
  - Make sure that you are only sewing those two layers and that nothing extra is slipping under the foot.
  - When sewing a curved seam or a seam that doesn't sit flat, make sure you pin well and sew it in small sections.

Tips

- *Having a speed control option on your machine is great, but try not to keep it on the slowest setting all the time as this can make your lines uneven. Increase the speed as you get more confident on the machine.*

- *Whether or not you have speed control on your sewing machine, you do not have to sew a row of stitching in one go. Sew a few centimetres, stop and check positioning, then continue.*

- *If you stop mid stitch line for any reason, hand-wind your needle down into the fabric so you do not lose your spot.*

What to do if you go off-track

- If you feel you are going off-track, do not take the needle up and out and reposition, as you will get a step in your stitch line. Instead, guide yourself back on track slowly and most of the time you will not even notice the slight kink in the line.

- If it is an obvious mistake, just unpick a few stitches on either side, take a deep breath and start again. It will get easier with practice!

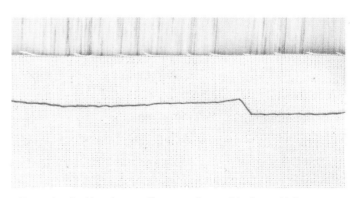

Example of taking the needle out and repositioning, which creates a step, which you don't want.

BACKSTITCHING AT THE END

- Always backstitch at the end of a straight row of stitching, when sewing a seam. You need only backstitch two or three stitches but this will secure your ends and stop your row of stitching from unravelling.

- Do not sew off the fabric. Always finish on the fabric.

- When you finish sewing, it is hugely important to hand-wind your needle out of the fabric and into the top position, as this will allow your machine to finish its cycle of sewing a stitch. (Some machines will do this automatically for you.) You can then release the fabric easily from the machine, allowing the threads to flow freely.

- If you don't wind your needle to the top position, you may have four threads coming out of the machine and you will be tugging at your fabric to remove it. Simply wind your needle to the top position and your fabric will come out smoothly.

Needle in top position.

Tip

- *Always leave the two ends long – 13cm (5⅛in) or longer. If you cut them too short after sewing, you will find that the thread slips out of your needle and will need rethreading.*

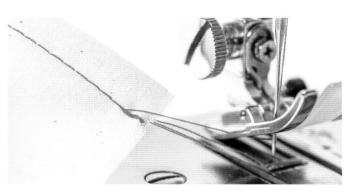

If four threads are visible, wind your needle to the top position.

PRESSING A SEAM

- Once you have finished sewing a seam, always press it open before moving on to the next stage. This makes for a much neater finish than trying to press every seam at the end.

- Use the tip of an iron on the inside of the seam to tease the seam open, then press with a bit of steam.

- Use an ironing ham to help iron curved seams.

- If you have creases in cotton fabrics, spray them with water from the iron and then, using steam, iron firmly over them.

- Try not to press from the outside of a garment over a lumpy seam, as this can sometimes leave an imprint. Try to iron within the seams.

- Do not spray satins as they will retain watermarks. If water gets on satin, apply the heat of the iron as soon as you can to dry it out. Otherwise, it will come out in the wash.

Your seams should be pressed open like this before joining your piece to the next one.

NEATENING THE SEAM

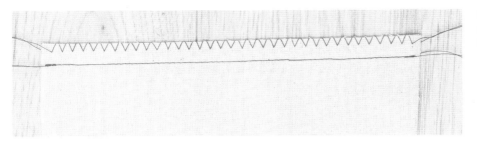

Once you have sewn and pressed a seam, you need to neaten the edge with zigzag stitch.

- To prevent your seams from unravelling, you will need to finish them, either using a zigzag stitch or an overlocker (serger). An overlocker (serger) gives a more professional finish but the easiest way to finish a seam is with zigzag stitch.

- You don't need to backstitch when zigzagging. You can cut your ends and tie them together for a neat and secure finish.

- You can zigzag stitch most seams together, but when a seam needs to open to allow for a zip fastening, you will need to neaten the seam allowances separately.

Sewing zigzag stitch

- Set your sewing machine stitch to zigzag.
  - Set the length to 2–3.
  - Set the width to 4–5.
- If you can't change the length and width, simply choose a long and wide zigzag stitch.)

- At the start of the seam, place your seam edge under the foot. Lower your foot and begin to zigzag, allowing the needle to miss the fabric on the right of each stitch. This means that the threads wrap around the seam edge to secure it. Adjust the positioning accordingly.

Tip
- Don't get too worried about the positioning of the zigzag stitch. A row of zigzag in some form is better than nothing at all.

LAST POINTS

- If your machine isn't working properly, there is usually a good reason, so unthread it, reinsert the bobbin and start again.
- If it still isn't working, find a friendly local shop to visit and ask for their help!
- Remember, if you have a decent machine, treat it well and it will last you a lifetime.

Once you get your head around this information, you are set to sew!

How to make this dress
This classic-style dress features slightly flared sleeves (see page 108), an A-line skirt with box pleats (page 132) and a 'V'-shaped neckline (page 95). I made it here in a printed cotton fabric for a daytime look, but you could turn it into a gorgeous evening dress by using a duchess satin.

fabrics

Your choice of fabric will be key when choosing the type of dress you want to make. There is a huge array of fabrics available to buy these days and it can all seem very overwhelming, so let me guide you through the basics in this section.

Your choice of fabric will completely change the look of a dress. When selecting your fabric, you will need to consider the following qualities: **type of fabric; cost; pattern; width; ease of handling; washing; comfort; structure and drape**.

Type of fabric

Natural   This means that the fabrics are created from natural sources, for example: cotton, denim, silk, linen and wool.

Synthetic   This means that the fabrics are created using man-made fibres, for example: polyester, nylon, acrylic, Spandex, jersey and microfibre.

Fabrics are either natural, synthetic or a combination of both so the qualities of the fabrics are combined. For example:

- **Cotton** is natural and is cool to wear, yet creases easily.
- **Polyester** is synthetic and is hot to wear, yet is crease-resistant.
- **Polycotton** is a mixture of the two to combine both qualities, so is cooler to wear than polyester and is more crease-resistant than 100% cotton. It is a very common fabric choice for clothing.

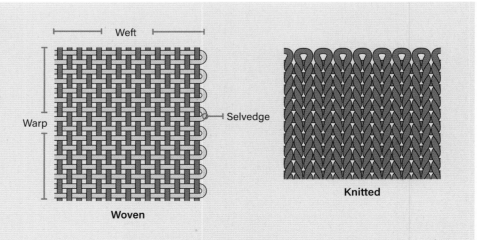

FABRIC STRUCTURE

Fabric is made up of fibres which are spun into yarns. Yarns are either woven together at right angles to each other, on a loom, to create more structured woven fabrics (right), or they can be knitted together by interlocking loops on a machine to create looser and stretchier fabrics (far right). See page 31 for a note on stretch fabrics.

Weft

Warp

Selvedge

Woven

Knitted

Cost

As with most things, you get what you pay for. Cheap fabric can be quite thin or stiff/starchy so is not always the best choice for clothing.

At the same time, you don't want to buy an expensive fabric and not get the fit right first. Choose a cheaper fabric such as calico to make a sample, or toile, first (see page 60). Then, when you have your pattern adjusted and ready to cut, you can measure exactly what you need and can then purchase your fabric.

You can buy fabric online but nothing beats going into a fabric store and seeing and feeling the fabric for yourself. You can take along a drawing or picture of what you have planned, and ask for help and advice on what is best.

Pattern

When choosing fabrics, you will obviously be considering the colour and maybe print of a fabric. When starting out in dressmaking, don't give yourself a hard task by choosing a pattern that you will want to 'pattern match' at the seams, like stripes or a repeated pattern. If you do need to do any pattern matching, you will usually require additional fabric, which is another thing to keep in mind.

I advise that you go for quite abstract patterns, such as florals. Start simple and you can then progress to more complicated ideas.

You will also need to consider if there is a direction to your pattern. You will need to make sure your pattern pieces are all placed on your fabric the same way up for continuity.

Width

You will need to know the width of fabric when purchasing it, to allow you to buy the correct amount for your garment. The most common widths of fabric are 115cm (45in) or 150cm (60in). Wider cottons are sometimes available.

- If you buy a narrow fabric, you will need to buy more of it than if you were to buy a wider fabric.
- When positioning a full dress pattern on fabric, it is useful to create a **layplan**, which is a plan for the positioning to get the most out of your fabric (see also page 60). Making sure you are economical with your fabric will save you from buying too much.

I will help you understand pattern positioning a bit further on (see pages 60–61).

Ease of handling

When starting out sewing, I would avoid anything shiny, stretchy or with sequins or beads. Keep it simple and then progress onto other fabrics as you get more confident.

- You want the fabric to be easy to handle when cutting out and also when sewing.
- You want to be able to lay your fabric easily without it moving too much when placing your pattern on top.
- You will want to be able to pin it easily when placing patterns and when pinning the seams together.
- Woven cotton and cotton mixes are usually the easiest fabrics to work with.

Washing

Think about how your fabric will wash and how it will be after a wash. Most fabrics will be washed at 30–40° C (86–104°F) in a washing machine. The 100% natural fabrics will crease so you will need to be prepared to iron them once dry. The synthetic and mixed fabrics will need less ironing after a wash.

- It is advisable to wash and dry your fabric before you cut out and make a garment, as some fabrics can shrink after a wash – not ideal once you've perfected the fit of your dream dress!
- The colour can run on some fabrics so a prewash will determine that. This helps if you plan to mix a few coloured fabrics.
- To be honest, I don't prewash everything as I mainly use high-quality printed cottons but it is your own choice.

If you do choose to prewash your fabric, make sure you wash an uncut length. Whatever you do, don't cut out your pieces and then wash them as they may shrink and most likely fray in the machine.

Ironing your fabric

• As a rule, I suggest setting your iron to 2 dots (medium temperature). Don't go any higher unless you are working with a natural fabric that needs the extra heat. I iron everything on 2 dots with steam to get any creases out. If you set the iron any higher, you may melt your fabric if it is synthetic, or burn it if it is natural.

Comfort

When choosing your fabric, feel both sides of it and hold it against your skin so that you know you will be comfortable when wearing it. Some fabrics can look beautiful but may be a bit harsh against your bare skin. Think about under your arms and around the neckline.

You can line a dress but it becomes a more advanced garment. I have kept it simple in this book and not included linings, so do make sure your fabrics feel comfortable.

Structure and drape

If you hold a piece of fabric out in front of you, it will hang in a particular way depending on how firm or soft it is (see below).

When you decide which style of dress you want to make, you should then pick your fabric to suit that shape and the drape you want.

FIRMER FABRICS

Firmer fabrics will be quite stiff and hang quite straight, therefore they will allow you to make a more structured garment which will hold its shape well.

Firmer fabrics work well for fitted styles, box pleats, A-line shapes and statement sleeves.

SOFTER FABRICS

Softer fabrics will be more flimsy and sometimes floaty, therefore they will allow you to make a garment which drapes more softly.

Softer fabrics work well for soft gathered pleats, full circle skirts and floaty sleeves.

My key fabrics

I have chosen to focus on seven fabrics that I recommend for dressmaking, as this will help those of you who are starting at the beginning. I've provided information on the most important qualities to look for (see pages 24–27) to help you make an informed decision.

1. CALICO – THE PERFECT PRACTICE FABRIC

Before you even think about which fabrics you want to use to make your first dress, I advise that you buy a small supply of a cotton fabric called calico. Calico can be used as a practice fabric as it is relatively cheap to buy, comes in a few thicknesses and you can easily manipulate it and draw on it. In the clothing industry, a practice/sample garment is called a toile and is made using calico. I highly recommend that you always make a sample, or toile, first to get the perfect fit to your dress. I will guide you through making your own sample (toile) on pages 60–73.

A mediumweight calico is ideal as it can be manipulated to fit the body and will hang nicely. It is the perfect weight to start you off, whichever style of dress you choose to make.

2. COTTON

Cotton comes in lots of thicknesses, giving you a few options as to how soft or structured you want your dress to be. It has some excellent qualities, which makes it one of my favourite fabrics to use for my style of dresses.

Type of fabric   Natural. Comes in a range of thicknesses.

Cost   Very affordable and readily available.

Width   Available in both 115cm (45in) and 150cm (60in).

Pattern   Available in all types of colourways and prints.

Ease of handling   Easy to handle and iron.

Washing   Easy to machine wash but will crease easily.

Comfort   Cool to wear. Soft against the skin and very comfortable.

Structure and drape   A lightweight cotton will allow you to make a soft summer dress whereas a heavier cotton will give you a more structured look for a fitted-style dress.

Tip

• Lightweight cottons are great for the softer style dress with a more floaty finish but be careful not to go too thin or the fabric will be see-through and harder to manage.

3. DENIM (A TYPE OF COTTON)

I adore denim as I just love how easy it is to handle. It usually irons beautifully and if used correctly, can allow you to create a beautifully structured dress.

Type of fabric   Natural. Comes in a range of thicknesses.

Cost   Very affordable and readily available.

Width   Available in both 115cm (45in) and 150cm (60in).

Pattern   Denim is traditionally blue and grey but is readily available in a wider range of colours these days. Denim is also available with prints on and embroidery.

Ease of handling   Easy to handle and iron.

Washing   Easy to machine wash but will crease easily.

Comfort   Cool to wear. Very comfortable and traditionally durable.

Structure and drape   A lightweight denim will allow you to make a softer style dress whereas a heavier denim will allow you to make a structured, fitted-style dress.

4. CREPE

Crepe is one of the softer, more floaty fabrics I would recommend. The right weight of crepe will allow you to make a dress which drapes beautifully and still has good body to it.

Type of fabric   Natural and also a mixed fabric. Comes in a few thicknesses.

Cost   Affordable and relatively easy to find.

Width   Available in both 115cm (45in) and 150cm (60in).

Pattern   Available in various colourways and prints.

Ease of handling   Easy to handle but seams can be a little bouncy when ironing and may not sit totally flat.

Washing   Easy to wash but will crease easily if 100% natural.

Comfort   Cool to wear if natural. Soft against the skin and very comfortable.

Structure and drape   A lightweight crepe will drape beautifully and a heavier crepe will still drape but will have a fuller feel to it.

Tips

- *Be careful not to get too thick a denim as it can be hard to sew thick layers with some domestic sewing machines.*
- *Colourful threads will allow you to sew a highlighted row of top-stitching along the seam.*

Tip

- *Make sure your needle is sharp, as crepe can snag easily.*

5. WOOL

Wool is a lovely fabric to work with for dressmaking. Heavier wools are commonly used for outerwear but if you find a lightweight wool, it can make a beautiful dress for the winter months.

Type of fabric   Natural. Woven wool will be more suitable for dressmaking. Knitted wool can be more stretchy.

Cost   Usually more expensive than cotton.

Width   Available in both 115cm (45in) and 150cm (60in).

Pattern   Available in a wide range of colours and patterns.

Ease of handling   Easy to handle but care must be taken when ironing. Iron on a low heat with a damp cloth if needed.

Washing   Needs to be prewashed to allow for shrinkage. Hand-washing or dry cleaning is recommended.

Comfort   Cool to wear if lightweight. It is best to line a wool garment as it may be a little scratchy against your skin.

Structure and drape   For dressmaking, I suggest a lightweight wool, which will give you an elegant drape.

6. POLYCOTTON

Polycotton is a perfect fabric to start your dressmaking journey with. A mixture of cotton and polyester, polycotton is durable and crease-resistant, meaning less ironing than 100% cotton! It is easy to handle and to get hold of and is available in an array of colours and patterns.

Type of fabric   Mixture of natural and synthetic. Comes in a range of thicknesses.

Cost   Very affordable and readily available.

Width   Available in both 115cm (45in) and 150cm (60in).

Pattern   Available in all types of colourways and prints.

Ease of handling   Crease-resistant, very easy to handle and iron.

Washing   Easy to machine wash.

Comfort   Soft against the skin and very comfortable to wear.

Structure and drape   Depends on the weight but it is usually used for a more structured style than floaty.

Tip

- *Use a ball-point needle as it has a rounded tip which slips easily through the fibres, so avoids snagging. You can try a normal needle also but sew a test piece first.*

Tip

- *Polycotton is very easy to manipulate so is perfect for pleating and shaping a garment.*

A WORD ABOUT STRETCH FABRICS

Stretch fabrics are fantastic to work with as you don't have to worry so much about the fit: your fabrics will stretch around your body. However, I don't recommend using stretch fabrics if you are new to sewing. It is best to fully understand the processes of pattern cutting and making a dress to fit you while using a fabric that is easy to handle.

If you are used to using stretch fabrics, I would recommend that you use a thick stretch fabric, so you can still make up the garments using the patterns in this book.

7. POLYESTER SATIN

If you would like your fabric to have a silky sheen, you do not need to get silk as it is expensive and difficult to handle. Polyester satin is an easier fabric to handle and will still give you a beautiful finish. I would avoid starting your dressmaking journey with satin, due to it being slippery to handle, but don't be afraid to try it once you get going.

Type of fabric   Mix of natural and synthetic. Comes in a range of thicknesses.

Cost   Very affordable and readily available.

Width   Available in both 115cm (45in) and 150cm (60in).

Pattern   Available in all types of colourways and prints.

Ease of handling   A little bit tricky to handle as its shiny surface makes it a bit slippery. It needs to be pinned well when sewing. Care must be taken when ironing also. Never more than 2 dots (medium temperature). Can be left with watermarks so beware of leaky irons!

Washing   Easy to wash but will need ironing.

Comfort   Soft against the skin and comfortable to wear.

Structure and drape   Depends on the weight, but polyester satin can be used to create a really stunning effect. A lighter weight satin will be harder to use but will drape well for a softer look, whereas a heavier 'duchess satin' will create a fabulous, well-structured dress.

Tip

• *Always test your needle before sewing satin as a blunt needle will snag your fabric. Even better, always put a new needle in when starting a new project.*

sewing language

what does it all mean?

Dressmaking may seem a little daunting at first but don't panic – I am going to explain exactly what you need to know to get started, beginning with some key sewing terminology.

Here are all the basic terms that I will be using throughout the book.

PATTERN PIECE

Think of a pattern like a jigsaw: a pattern includes a set of several **pieces**, which when put together correctly, will make a garment in a particular size. Pattern pieces are created on paper or card, following the measurements of the body.

Every item of clothing is comprised of a set of unique pattern pieces in a set size, which, when cut out in fabric and sewn together, make the finished garment.

BLOCK

Our **block** comprises a set of five basic pattern pieces, which when sewn together, make up a simple dress. These pattern pieces are used as a basis to start from, and are then altered to make your garment to your exact size and taste. The five basic pattern pieces in this block are a front bodice, back bodice, front skirt, back skirt and sleeve.

A block will come in a set for each size based on a size chart. The size chart in this book is not based on European, American or UK dress-size conventions. Instead, the sizes start at 1 and go up to 19; they are universal, bespoke and user-friendly. (See page 45.)

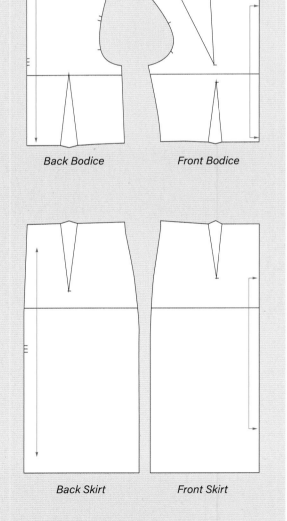

Back Bodice   *Front Bodice*

Back Skirt   *Front Skirt*

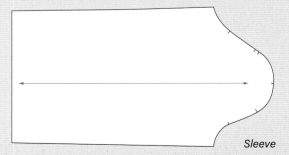

Sleeve

GRADED NEST OF PATTERNS

A graded nest of patterns consists of each of the five block pattern pieces, individually scaled up and down to other sizes, using a technical process called 'grading'.

Each pattern piece has its own nest and its own set of rules applied to scale it up or down to the next pattern size. You will find a graded nest for each of the five block pattern pieces on the pattern sheets in the envelope inside this book. You will have a set of nests for sizes 1 to 9 and another set of nests for sizes 10 to 19. Each size is colour-coded: for instance, size 1 is denoted by fuchsia lines, size 9 by light blue; size 10 by light green lines, and size 19 is denoted by purple lines. This colour-coding will help you trace off the correct block for your size each time.

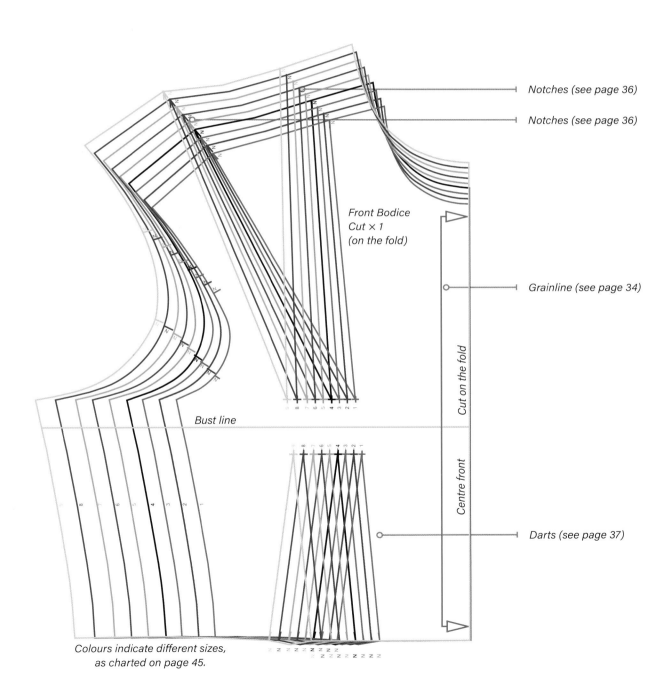

Notches (see page 36)

Notches (see page 36)

Front Bodice
Cut × 1
(on the fold)

Grainline (see page 34)

Cut on the fold

Bust line

Centre front

Darts (see page 37)

Colours indicate different sizes, as charted on page 45.

PATTERN CUTTING

Pattern cutting is the process of creating or drafting a pattern for a garment using body measurements and mathematics, either from scratch or by adapting an existing pattern. Pattern cutting will allow you to adapt the blocks supplied with this book to fit your body and to create a garment that is unique to you. You can then alter your pattern further by changing the neckline, length, sleeve details, fit etc. This is all done on paper using various pattern-cutting techniques.

There is a lot to learn and, yes, mathematics plays a big part, but I will guide you through the basics as gently as possible. Having the recommended tools handy will make it all a lot easier and quicker.

PATTERN MARKINGS

Every pattern piece will need to have a range of pattern markings on it. These detailed markings will guide you when you cut out your fabric and help when you sew up your garment. It is good to get used to certain terms and try to make sure your patterns are well labelled, as it really will help you.

Grainlines

These are so important! Every pattern piece should have a grainline on it, which is marked as a straight line with an arrow at one or each end. The grainline tells you how to position the pattern piece on the fabric, to match the grain of the fabric.

Unfortunately, with clothing, you can't just place the pattern piece any way around on the fabric as this really will affect the way the garment sits and how easy it is to construct. Let me tell you why in the simplest way possible...

Understanding the grain

Get yourself some firm (not stretchy), preferably cotton fabric that you plan to use. Place it in front of you as you read this.

- *When fabric is on a roll, at each side of the roll is the selvedge/selvage edge, which means 'self-finished'. This will be perfectly straight and uncut, so will not fray or unravel. This sometimes has the designer or fabric's name written on, or colour tests printed on.*

- *Holding that piece of fabric firmly in each hand, pull the fabric along the length of the selvedge. It should be quite firm. This is called the 'straight of grain'.*

- *Then, pull it in the opposite direction across the fabric, from selvedge to selvedge. It should also be quite firm. This is called straight of grain as well, but is also referred to as the cross grain.*

- *Now pull your fabric apart diagonally and you will notice that the fabric stretches. This is called the bias. Patterns are cut on the bias when soft drape is desired.*

- *If the garment is fitted and needs some structure, the grainline will be on the straight of grain to allow a good fit and ease of construction. In this book, all of the pattern pieces will be cut on the straight of grain, as shown here.*

The main rule, when placing a pattern piece onto fabric, is that the grainline should always either be parallel to the selvedge or at 90 degrees to it, as shown opposite.

Whichever way you place your patterns, just make sure all of the pattern pieces are going in the same direction and the grainlines are all placed in the same way for continuity.

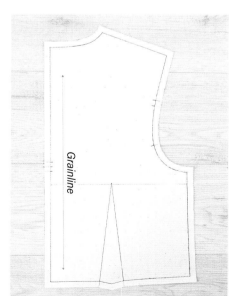

Grainline

The selvedge.

The straight of grain.

The bias.

Grainline is at 90 degrees to the selvedge.

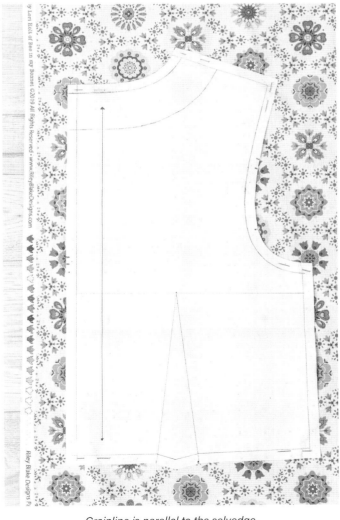

Grainline is parallel to the selvedge.

Notches (my favourite things!)

These need to be accurate! Notches are vital to a pattern as they help you match up each pattern piece precisely. They are typically recognized as little triangles on older style patterns, or as small lines on more modern patterns (as shown in this book). They really will help you when constructing a garment as, without them, you will be guessing where your patterns meet along the seam edges, which can throw out the fit of a garment completely.

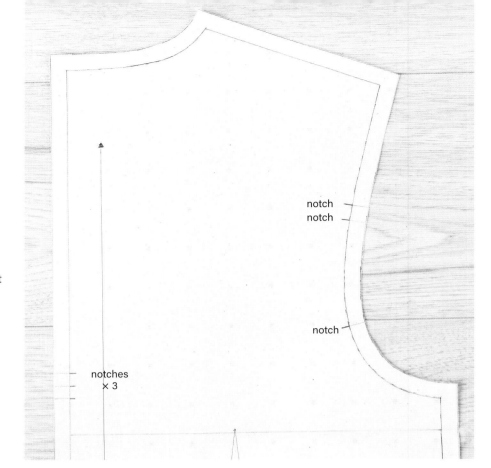

notch

notch

notch

notches × 3

Seam allowance

This needs to be accurate. The seam allowance on a pattern piece is another important marking (see page 18). A pattern master ruler will really help you draw your seam allowances quickly and accurately. I tend to work with a 1cm (⅜in) seam allowance, but you can make it 1.5cm (⅝in) if you prefer a bigger seam allowance. Make sure you set yourself up for the correct seam allowance when sewing.

Note that although I prefer a 1cm (⅜in) seam allowance in general, I recommend a 1.5cm (⅝in) seam allowance on the seam where the zip will be placed, which is usually the centre-back seam.

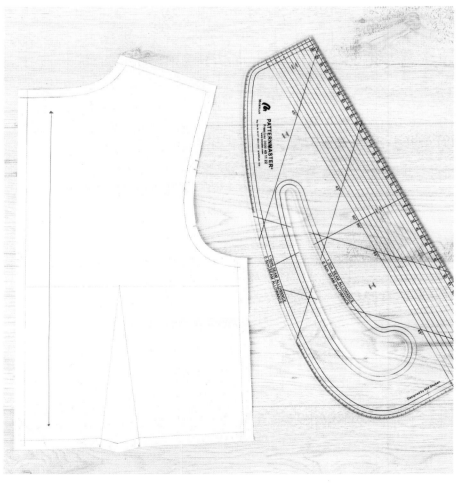

Darts

These give the shape. Darts are a way of manipulating fabric to give a three-dimensional shape to a flat pattern piece. They are shown on a pattern piece as a 'V' shape. The 'V'-shaped dart is sewn together on the inside of the garment so it is not visible on the outside. Instead, a simple straight seam line is seen and shape is created.

Darts are used on curvy areas of the body such as the bust, hips and waist. They are not as scary as you may think. See pages 64–68 for information on sewing darts.

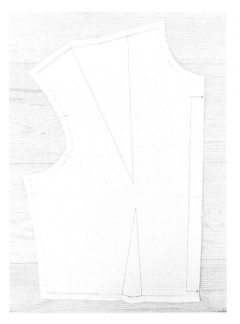
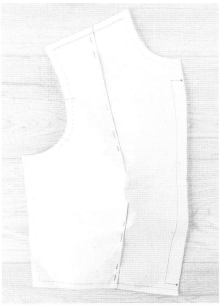

Flat pattern piece.

Pattern piece with darts pinned to create a three-dimensional shape.

PLEATS

These are the fun bits! Pleats are folds in the fabric which are secured in place to create fullness and structure in a garment. Pleats will reduce the width of your fabric but also create volume.

You can create narrow little pleats such as pin tucks or create more of a feature using a box pleat. You can have fun with pleats on skirts especially, but you can also use them in other areas of a garment, such as the sleeve. See pages 132–134.

Find out how to make the box-pleated skirt shown here on page 132.

These pleats are called 'box pleats'.

FASTENINGS

Garments can be fastened in a number of ways, using zips, buttons, hooks-and-eyes, ties and so on, or they may be loose enough that they don't need a fastening at all. For the garments in this book we'll be using zips.

There are two methods of attaching zips to choose from in this book: choose from a lapped zip or a concealed zip.

As with most things, you just need to practise the techniques involved – zips are easy when you know how. See pages 146–153.

Zips tend to scare a lot of people as a badly inserted zip can look a little unsightly. I know, as I had that fear back when I was a student! With a bit of practice and patience, however, a neatly inserted zip completes a garment and gives a professional finish.

A concealed zip in place on a skirt.

FACINGS

The professional finish. Facings take your garment to the next level of professional! They are only seen on the inside of a garment but they help to finish it off neatly and can also add a little more structure. I like to think that the inside of the garment is as important as the outside, especially when I design and create beautiful wedding gowns. You should be proud of what you make, so the finish is everything. I once had the amazing compliment that one of my wedding dresses could be worn inside out as it looked so beautiful and neat.

When you are starting out, everything will take time to master but to strive for a neat finish will make the whole process much more rewarding.

Above, neckline facings on the inside from the back (left) and the front (right) of a dress.

How to make this outfit

This simple A-line skirt has added box pleats to give it more shape (see page 132). A waistband allows the skirt to sit neatly on the waist (page 156). I made it in a printed cotton fabric for a comfortable daywear look. The simple top (page 154) has a curved neckline (page 94) and beautiful capped sleeves (page 110). The skirt could be made in a denim to give a much more structured look, and could be paired with a soft printed cotton or even polyester satin top to really ring the changes.

GETTING STARTED

1 sizing

'Size' can be a scary word when it comes to dressmaking as we are all unique in body shape and size. Of all the women I have made clothes for over the years – and I am talking a lot of women – no two of them have been the same size.

There are no set sizing standards in the UK these days so every shop you visit will have its own set of sizes, which is why you can be a UK size 10 in one shop and a size 14 in another.

I am going to help you create a pattern that is as perfect a fit as possible for you. I will help you find the size nearest to your unique measurements, and we will work on altering the pattern to fit you accordingly. Just remember, women are beautiful in all shapes and sizes!

How to measure

You will need a tape measure, a full-length mirror, a pen and some paper to jot down your measurements. Having someone to help you measure yourself is always handy.

Wear thin clothing to measure over or put some pretty underwear on for the occasion. Put on your normal, everyday bra, as this will reflect your true shape.

When measuring yourself, don't pull the tape measure too tight. Hold two fingers under the tape measure, between the tape and your body: you don't want your pattern to be too figure-hugging and therefore too small. Do *not* hold your breath!

Write down the measurement in centimetres to the nearest millimetre (you can measure in inches if you prefer). Just be as accurate as you can, and definitely don't round it down!

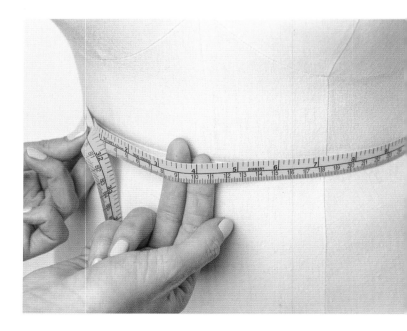

Key measurements

The main measurements you need are your bust, waist and hips.

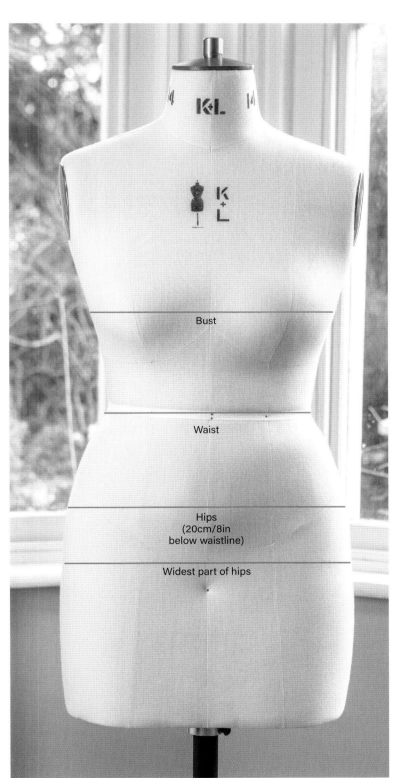

Bust

Waist

Hips
(20cm/8in
below waistline)

Widest part of hips

Bust   The measurement around the fullest part of your bust. Keep the measuring tape straight over the bust and around the back. Make sure it does not slip off the bust.

Waist   The measurement of the narrowest part of the body. Close your eyes and put your hands on your waist and this is usually the right spot. Otherwise, tie a piece of string or elastic around your waist or put on a narrow belt as this will work its way naturally to the narrowest part.

Hips   The hip measurement is taken 20cm (8in) below the waist measurement.

Widest part of hips   If your hips are wider below the 20cm (8in) hip mark, measure the widest part and also measure how far down that measurement sits.

Sizing tips

- *We need to accept what we are born with and learn to accentuate our best bits (and other bits too!) as this is what makes us unique.*

- *The key to it all is dressing for your shape and feeling good in what you wear, as you will then radiate confidence.*

- *Size is just a number. Make sure you work out your actual dress size from the chart and be true to yourself as you want your dresses to fit you.*

- *Be realistic with sizing as it is better to take in something that is too big than try to fit into something that is too small.*

USEFUL EXTRA MEASUREMENTS

These measurements are useful to refer to when you have your pattern pieces in front of you. You won't need them when choosing your size pattern from my blocks, so if you want to keep it simple, stick with the bust, waist and hip measurements for now.

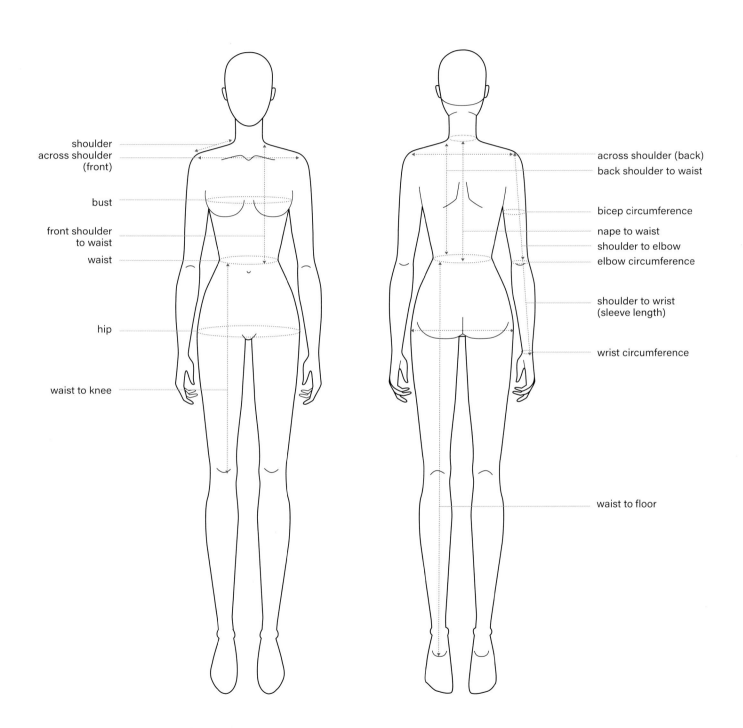

shoulder
across shoulder (front)
bust
front shoulder to waist
waist
hip
waist to knee

across shoulder (back)
back shoulder to waist
bicep circumference
nape to waist
shoulder to elbow
elbow circumference
shoulder to wrist (sleeve length)
wrist circumference
waist to floor

Noting your measurements

Fill in the blank table below with your own measurements. Measure in centimetres or inches, but not a combination of both!

KEY MEASUREMENTS
Bust
Waist
Hips

USEFUL EXTRA MEASUREMENTS
Front shoulder to waist
Back shoulder to waist
Shoulder
Across shoulder (front)
Across shoulder (back)
Shoulder to elbow
Shoulder to wrist (sleeve length)
Elbow to wrist
Bicep circumference
Elbow circumference
Wrist circumference
Widest part of hips (≥20cm/8in) below hipline *Waist to widest part of hips*
Waist to knee
Waist to floor

Now you have your measurements, keep them safe, make a cup of tea and take your time reading the next section before you do anything else. This is where you will choose your pattern sizes.

How to make this dress
This dress consists of a crepe bodice with a high curved neckline (see page 94) and soft capped sleeves (page 110). The bodice is attached to a fitted skirt (page 122), which is in a contrasting floral cotton fabric. The floral collar (page 136) really pulls the look together to make a fun and vibrant dress. You could make the dress in a mediumweight black wool, to create a stylish little black dress.

Understanding ease

Before we look at the size chart, we need to talk about **ease**. Ease is the difference between the measurements of your own body and the **actual finished measurements** of a garment.

Ease in a garment is essential, especially when using fabrics which are not stretchy, as it allows ease of movement. Without ease in the garment, it will be skin-tight, meaning you will not be able to reach, bend, sit or move easily.

There are two types of ease: **wearing ease** and **design ease**. **Wearing ease** is the amount of ease in a garment to allow you to move freely whilst wearing it. For example, a fitted dress will have wearing ease worked into the pattern but will still accentuate the figure.

Design ease is the amount of ease added into a garment to allow for a loose-fitting design. For example, a loose fitting A-line dress will have a lot more ease to allow for a relaxed fit on the waist and hips.

We will focus on the wearing ease when creating our first blocks as the idea is to create a block that fits you. You can adjust the design, fit and style later on.

You will need to add wearing ease onto your body measurements, using the Wearing Ease Guide on the right. The tips below will help you work out how much to add.

WEARING EASE GUIDE

Bust	Add 5–10cm (2–4in)
Waist	Add 1–4cm (½–1½in)
Hips	Add 5–10cm (2–4in)

KEY MEASUREMENTS		+ wearing ease
Bust		
Waist		
Hips		

Tips

- *If you want your sample (toile) to be quite fitted, go with the minimal amount of ease, whereas if you want a looser fit, add more.*
- *The larger the size, the more ease you should add.*
- *To help you choose the amount of ease to add, you can add the minimum ease to your measurement and put the tape measure around you to see how loosely it fits around you.*
- *Just remember, it is always better to add too much as it is much easier to take in your sample (toile) than to add to it.*

Choosing the right size blocks

Keep your measurements to hand for this next section.

The next stage is choosing the right size pattern blocks to work with, based on your measurements.

Our bodies do not necessarily match one size only; if you are curvy, your hips are likely to be a different size from your waist and bust, so you will need to select the closest pattern size to your bust, waist and hips individually. On page 40, I will give you two examples to help you make your choice.

Once you have added wearing ease onto your bust, waist and hip measurements, you can then identify the pattern sizes nearest to your measurements on the size chart, opposite.

IMPORTANT: Choose the size nearest your bust or a size bigger as you want to get the best fit on the bust and to avoid trying to alter the darts. It is easier to alter the waist and hips.

The size chart

The sizes on the size chart below represent the **actual finished measurement** (that is, your measurements plus wearing ease), so you will need to have added wearing ease to your measurements before picking your size.

I have created a bespoke size chart which is purely based on measurements, making it universal. **There is no reference to UK, US or EU sizing**. You are unique in your size, so just choose the numbers nearest to your key measurements.

When choosing your sizes, if you are 1cm (⅜in) away from a given size, below, you can either circle the smaller or the bigger size adjacent.

If you are over 1cm (⅜in) from a set size, always go with the nearest, bigger size. We will be altering the pattern to fit you and it is always easier to take away from, rather than to add, to a pattern. (You will find this phrase repeated throughout the book!)

The following pages feature two real-life examples to help you choose your own sizes, so feel free to read through the examples to help you make sense of the process before you select your own size.

SIZES 1 TO 9

Size	1	2	3	4	5	6	7	8	9
Bust (cm)	79	84	89	94	99	104	109	115	121
Bust (in)	31⅛	33⅛	35	37	39	41	43	45¼	47⅝
Waist (cm)	61	66	71	76	81	86	91	97	103
Waist (in)	24	26	28	30	31⅞	33⅞	35⅞	38¼	40⅝
Hips (cm)	87	92	97	102	107	112	117	123	129
Hips (in)	34¼	36¼	38¼	40⅛	42⅛	44⅛	46⅛	48½	50¾

SIZES 10 TO 19

Size	10	11	12	13	14	15	16	17	18	19
Bust (cm)	127	133	140	147	154	161	168	175	182	189
Bust (in)	50	52⅜	55⅛	57⅞	60⅝	63⅜	66⅛	68⅞	71⅝	74⅜
Waist (cm)	109	115	122	129	136	143	150	157	164	171
Waist (in)	42⅞	45¼	48	50¾	53½	56⅜	59	61⅞	64⅝	67⅜
Hips (cm)	135	141	148	155	162	169	176	183	190	197
Hips (in)	53⅛	55½	58¼	61	63¾	66½	69¼	72	74¾	77½

Sizing in practice

Here, two of my pattern testers share their measurements, and I explain how we selected the correct-size blocks to trace off.

We chose to add a small amount of ease for the smaller sizes and increased the ease allowance as the sizes went up.

MARTINA

Bust: 121cm (47⅝in) + 10cm (4in) wearing ease = 131cm (51⅝in)
Waist: 114cm (44⅞in) + 4cm (1⅝in) wearing ease = 118cm (46½in)
Hips: 129cm (50¾in) + 10cm (4in) wearing ease = 139cm (54¾in)

Size chart	10		11		12
Bust (cm)	127	131 → *133*			140
Bust (in)	50		52⅜		55⅛
Waist (cm)	109		115	118 → *122*	
Waist (in)	42⅞		45¼		48
Hips (cm)	135	139 → *141*			148
Hips (in)	53⅛		55½		58¼

Based on Martina's measurements, we rounded up to Size 11 for her bust and opted to add 4cm (1⅝in) into the waist to allow for a comfortable fit, choosing Size 12. See page 56, 'Alteration technique: Adding onto the waist.'

Another option would have been to trace off the complete Size 12 Block and then take in the patterns to fit once a sample (toile) is made up.

LINDY

Bust: 129cm (50¾in) + 10cm (4in) wearing ease = 139cm (54¾in)
Waist: 124cm (48⅞in) + 4cm (1⅝in) wearing ease = 128cm (50½in)
Hips: 150cm (59⅛in)+ 10cm (4in) wearing ease = 160cm (63⅛in)

Size chart	10	11		12		13		14
Bust (cm)	127	133	139 → *140*			147		154
Bust (in)	50	52⅜		55⅛		57⅞		60⅝in
Waist (cm)	109	115		122	128 → *129*			136
Waist (in)	42⅞	45¼		48		50¾		53½
Hips (cm)	135	141		148		155	160 → *162*	
Hips (in)	53⅛	55½		58¼		61		63¾

Lindy wanted a comfortable fit without anything feeling tight so, based on her measurements, we decided to go one size bigger for the bust and trace off the complete Size 13 Block; we could then alter the side seams and hips to perfect the fit. See page 57, 'Alteration technique: Taking off the bodice side seams & adding onto the hips.' It is always easier to take in than to add to a bodice block.

Lindy took off 4cm (1⅝in) from the bodice side seams and added 5cm (2in) onto the hips at the hip line.

How to make this dress
This floaty dress is a combination of a bodice with a sweetheart neckline (see page 96) with butterfly sleeves (page 116), and a gorgeous full circle skirt (page 128). This is one of my favourite styles to wear with a full underskirt, and it also looks fabulous in a fabric like satin for a special event or night out.

2 pattern cutting

You should now have chosen your pattern sizes, using your measurements, so you are ready for this chapter.

Understanding the nest of patterns

Contained within this book, there are two sets of graded pattern nests printed full-size on pattern sheets: sizes 1 to 9, and sizes 10 to 19. You will need to open these out on a big table or the floor.

The blocks comprise the **Front Bodice, Back Bodice, Front Skirt, Back Skirt** and **Sleeve**. Familiarize yourself with each piece so you can clearly identify the size or sizes you will be tracing.

PREPARING TO TRACE YOUR PATTERNS

There are three methods for tracing off a pattern:

Method 1   Place some plain paper on top of the chosen nest and secure it with a few pins in each corner so it does not slip. Hopefully if your paper is not too thick, you can see the lines underneath and you can copy your chosen size (see overleaf).

Method 2   If you are lucky enough to own a decent-sized lightbox, you can secure your plain paper on top of the nest, and place both pieces on the lightbox to help you see the lines.

Method 3   If you struggle to see the lines, place the plain paper underneath the nest and secure it in place with pins. Then you can use a pattern tracer to carefully draw along the size pattern you want, and it will leave a line of small holes. Remove the nest, then join up the dots.

- Always use a sharp pencil, not a pen. Copy every line and marking on the block, even if you don't know what it means yet.

- Prepare to trace one pattern piece at a time. Cut a piece of paper at least 5cm (2in) bigger than the pattern piece so you have enough room around the pattern piece to add seam allowances and amend the pattern piece if you need to.

- Repeat this for each of the four pattern pieces of the block that we will be using – not the sleeve.

Note

Your sample will be made without a sleeve so that the fit can be perfected first – we will come back to the sleeve on page 82.

Remember...

- *The blocks will not fit you perfectly at this point and there is no seam allowance. You are just preparing the pieces for the next stage.*

- *You may need to trace off more than one size block if you are between sizes. You can either trace both sizes separately or, trace both sizes at the same time onto the same piece of paper so you can compare them.*

- *You will need to be as accurate as possible when tracing patterns as you can very easily lose or add 1cm (⅜in) or more if you are just off the line on every piece. Instructions for tracing off a pattern accurately are shown opposite.*

HOW TO TRACE OFF A PATTERN ACCURATELY

1 When your pattern is pinned in place, start by marking each significant point, like corner points, start and end of darts, centre line and grainline.

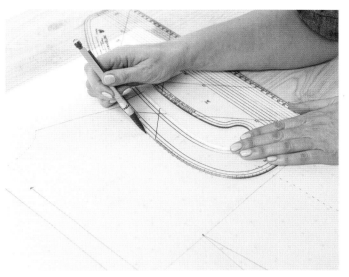

2 Now trace off the outline of the whole pattern piece. For straight lines, mark each end and join them with a ruler. Don't assume all lines are straight. For curves, draw a run of short, dashed pencil lines rather than one continuous line, then join the dashes using a curved ruler.

3 For the busy bits where it can be hard to define which line you want, lift the edges of the paper to double check which lines you are following. If you are still a bit unsure, just keep within the range of lines as best you can.

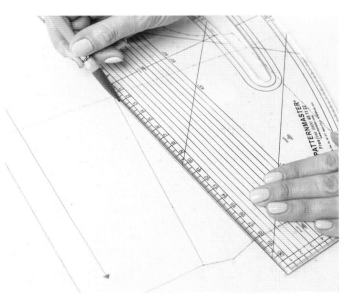

4 Mark in the crosses at the points of the darts and the base notches. Then draw in the straight lines of each dart using a ruler.

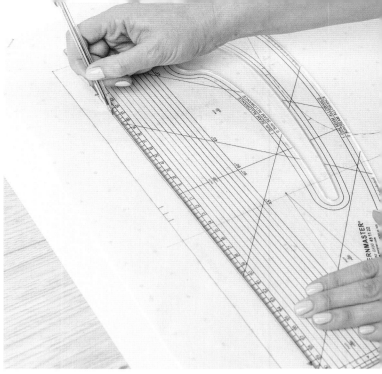

5 Make sure you copy over all notches as these are hugely important for the ease of construction.

6 Draw in the grainline, using a red pen if you have one.

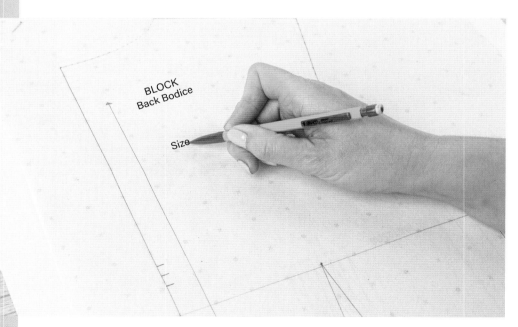

BLOCK
Back Bodice

Size

7 Label the pattern piece with the word BLOCK, piece name and size. Label each line to help you understand your pattern piece, for example, side seam, waistline, bust line, centre front, centre back, neckline, shoulder and so on.

See opposite for an example of a fully-labelled block of pattern pieces.

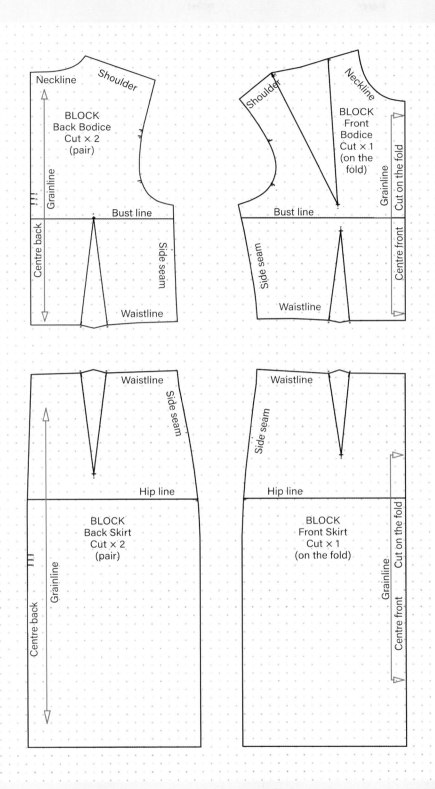

Now you have got your four block pattern pieces traced in the sizes needed, you will now need to alter them to fit you. Make a cup of tea, then start on the next chapter.

3 adjusting your blocks

You should now have your four block pattern pieces traced in the size you need.

When you have finished tracing off your chosen size, you will need to make some alterations to the blocks before making up your sample (toile).

In this chapter, I show you how to get the sizing of your blocks as accurate as possible by altering your pattern pieces accordingly. Every millimetre counts so be as precise as you can when altering your patterns.

Please remember that you always need to make a sample (toile) in fabric to see exactly how the garment will fit on you.

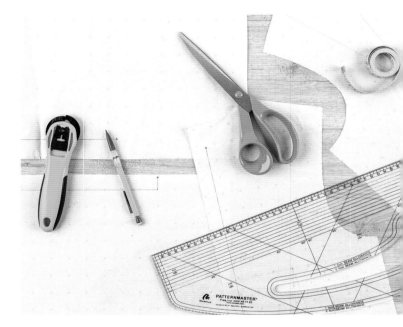

START AT THE TOP OF THE BODY

- **Do not touch any of the bust measurements, darts or armholes at this stage.** You should have chosen the size nearest your bust or a size bigger, so you don't need to alter it until your sample (toile) is made up.
- **Check the shoulder measurement.** If you have narrow shoulders, you might want to take off anything from 5mm (¼in) to 1.5cm (⅝in) from the outside shoulder. Just make sure the armhole remains exactly the same length:
- **Don't worry about adjusting the neckline yet:** it is useful to fit the sample (toile) with a high neck, so that your blocks fit your basic body. We can then alter the necklines later to accommodate the different design options (see pages 92–103).

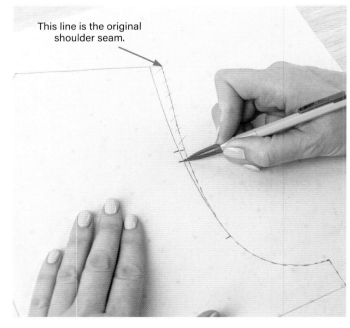

This line is the original shoulder seam.

If you are tall...

If you are tall (which in the UK means you are over 170cm, or 5ft 7in, tall), you should consider adding in anything up to 2.5cm (1in) at the waist on both the Front and Back Bodice blocks. Repeat the following steps on both bodice patterns.

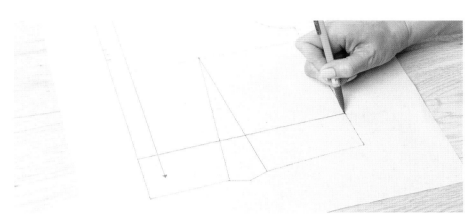

1 Draw a line approximately 5cm (2in) above the waistline and make sure it is as straight as possible, 90 degrees to the centre-front/centre-back edge.

2 Cut along this line to split your pattern into two pieces.

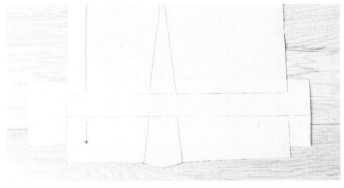

3 Stick a piece of pattern paper onto the cut end of the uppermost pattern piece, using masking or paper tape – sticking it to the back means you can still see the pattern line. Draw a parallel line to the cut line, the amount you want to extend your pattern by.

4 Extend the centre-front/centre-back edge to use as a marker to help realign your patterns.

5 Place the cut edge of the lower section of your pattern onto the new drawn line, lining up the centre-front/centre-back line. Stick it in place.

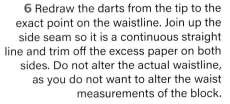

6 Redraw the darts from the tip to the exact point on the waistline. Join up the side seam so it is a continuous straight line and trim off the excess paper on both sides. Do not alter the actual waistline, as you do not want to alter the waist measurements of the block.

If you are petite…

If you are petite (which in the UK means you are under 160cm, or 5ft 3in, tall), you should consider taking up to 2.5cm (1in) off at the waist on the bodice blocks, or more if you need to.

1–2

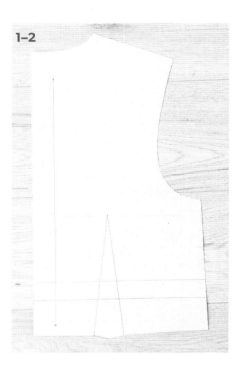

3

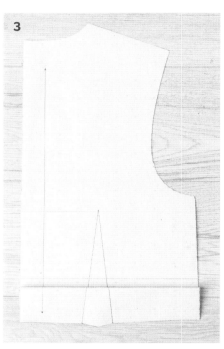

1 Draw a line approximately 5cm (2in) above the waistline and make sure it is as straight as possible, 90 degrees to the centre-front/centre-back edge.

2 Draw another line above, the amount you want to reduce the pattern by. Make sure both lines are parallel to each other.

3 Fold along the first line and then place the fold onto the second line, thus reducing the length in the bodice. Tape in place.

4 Redraw any lines that are not quite straight, including the side seam and darts. Do not alter the actual waistline as you do not want to alter the waist measurements of the block.

4

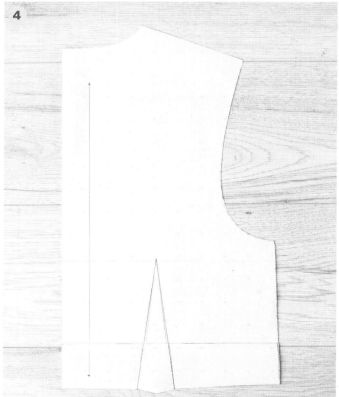

Tip

- *If you use a wheelchair, like my pattern tester Rhian, you will need to shorten the Front Bodice blocks and lengthen the Back Bodice blocks, to allow for a more comfortable fit.*

Altering the waist and hips

If you are a different size at the waist and/or hips to the bust, then you will need to alter the bodice blocks and skirt blocks accordingly.

Below are a few examples of the alterations you may need to make.

- When altering the patterns, try to make the lines as natural as possible with a gentle curve. Our bodies don't have corners and straight lines, so always think 'gentle curve.'

- Always make sure the same-size darts are used on the bodice and the skirt blocks so they are in line with each other on your garment. So, if you have traced a Size 12 bodice and a Size 14 skirt, make sure the Size 12 darts are also copied onto your pattern to match the bodice.

ALTERATION TECHNIQUE: ADDING ONTO THE HIPS

This alteration is for when the hips are bigger than the bust and waist measurements. To demonstrate this, I have used the Size 8 Block for the bust and waist and Size 9 Block for the bigger hip measurement.

1 Trace off both sizes of the Front and Back Skirt Blocks (and Bodice Blocks), on the same piece of paper. Here, the Size 8 block is purple; the Size 9 is blue.

2 The smaller size waist (Size 8) remains unchanged. From the Size 8 waist, draw a new line down to meet the bigger Size 9 hip line on both front and back side seams (shown in red).

3 Keep the waist darts at the smaller size, 8, so that they match the bodice at the waistline.

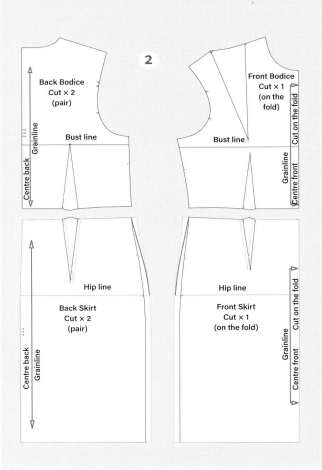

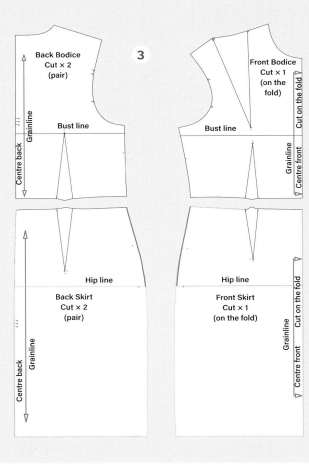

ALTERATION TECHNIQUE:
ADDING ONTO THE WAIST

This alteration applies when the pattern waist needs to be enlarged. This alteration was carried out for Martina's dress based on her measurements – see page 46.

- To demonstrate this, I have chosen to add 4cm (1½in) to the waist measurement (in the diagram below).

- Remember that your blocks are only half of your pattern. So, if you add 1cm (⅜in) onto your back side seam, you will actually be adding 2cm (¾in) in total to that piece once it is cut out as a 'left' half and a 'right' half.

- Therefore, to alter the side seams, you need to divide the amount you want to add/take away between all four side seams: Front Left, Back Left, Front Right and Back Right. I have added 1cm (⅜in) onto each side seam to total 4cm (1½in).

Tip

- *Make sure you alter both the bodice block and the skirt block, so that they match at the waist.*

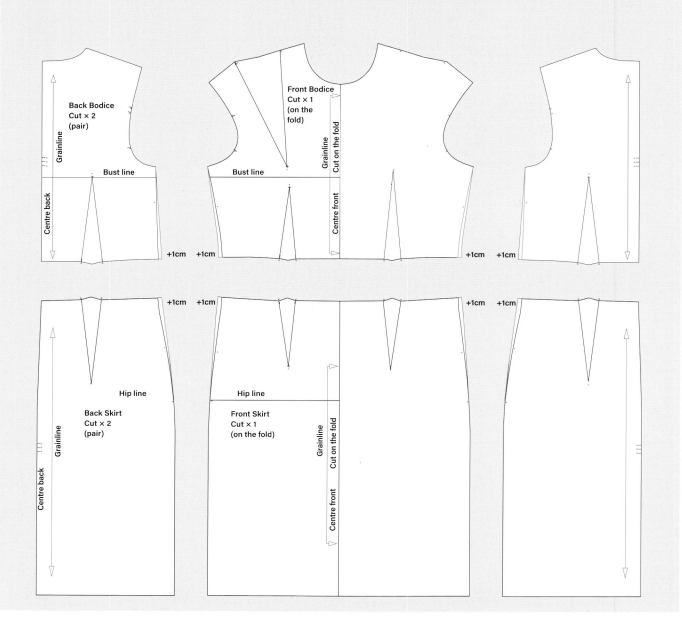

ALTERATION TECHNIQUE: TAKING OFF THE BODICE SIDE SEAMS & ADDING ONTO THE HIPS

This alteration applies when the bust and waist measurements are smaller than the hips. This alteration was carried out for Lindy's dress based on her measurements – see page 46.

- To demonstrate this, I have chosen the size nearest to the bust and waist measurement. The waist is the correct size whereas the bust side seams need reducing and the hips need extra.

- For example, if you need to take off 4cm (1½in) in total from the bust side seams, you need to take off 1cm (⅜in) from each individual seam. Take the full 1cm (⅜in) off at the top of the bodice side seams and graduate it down to the waist.

- Then, for example, if you need to add 5cm (2in) onto the hips at the hip line, add 1.25cm (½in) onto each individual seam. Graduate it up to nothing at the waist.

  It is important not to touch the darts!

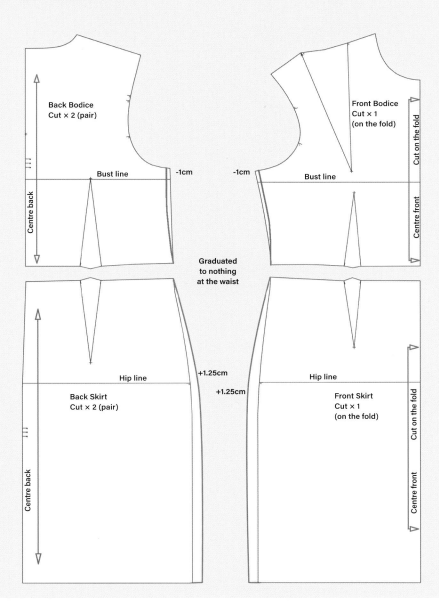

Altering the length of the skirt

At this stage, you can concentrate on the fit of the toile on the body and keep the length of the skirt as it is. When you try on your finished toile, you can decide on the style of skirt you would like to make. Then, you can see whether you might want to shorten the hem or lengthen it.

Whether you add onto the hem to lengthen it or take away some length to shorten it, just make sure you alter the hem with the exact same measurement the whole way around. Also, remember to allow for a turning allowance for the hem.

Adding seam allowances

Personally, I like to add 1cm (⅜in) seam allowances to my patterns as standard but if you want to make sure you have a bit extra within your seams, add a 1.5cm (⅝in) seam allowance. Note what you have added on the pattern pieces.

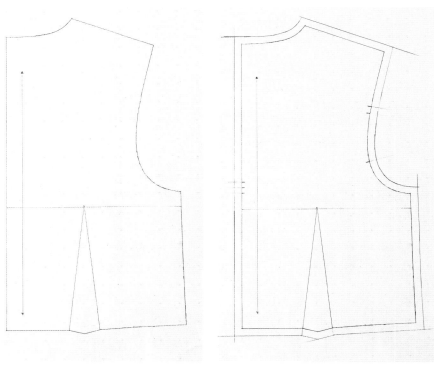

Back Bodice pattern before the seam allowance has been added.

Back Bodice pattern with a 1cm (⅜in) seam allowance added all the way around.

If you do not have a pattern master, you will need to use a tape measure or ruler and measure 1cm (⅜in) or 1.5cm (⅝in) from the edge of the design line, as accurately as possible. You will need to add a seam allowance the whole way around each pattern piece, following the shape of the block exactly. Do not add seam allowances to edges that are cut on the fold – i.e. the centre-front bodice edge and centre-front skirt edge.

Adding seam allowance at the base of a dart needs to be accurate. Extend the lines of the dart into the seam allowance and copy the shape of the base exactly.

Completed Back Bodice pattern piece with a 1cm (⅜in) seam allowance added.

Adding markings to the patterns

Make sure all of the notches are marked on the seam allowance and the base of the darts. You will need to extend the line of the notch to reach the edge of the pattern piece using a ruler. Make sure it is in line with the original notch.

Once you have cut out your pattern piece, you can use a notcher, shown right, if you have one, to mark your notches on the paper pattern. If you don't have a notcher, you can snip partway into the seam allowance of the paper pattern with scissors, or just leave notch markings as they are.

CUTTING OUT YOUR PAPER PATTERN PIECES

When you are happy with the alterations, the next step is cutting out your pattern pieces. Make sure you cut right alongside the pencil line of the seam allowance, so you can always see the original line as reference.

• Don't cut any further away from the line as the excess will increase the size of your pattern pieces.

• Equally, try not to cut inside the pencil line as you will lose that line; the more you use the pattern pieces, the more you risk trimming the pattern down.

• Write the following on the front of an envelope of roughly A4 size (29.7 × 21cm/11¾ × 8¼in): **Your name / Block pattern / First draft / The date / Seam allowance amount** (this is optional but can be helpful).

Keep all of your pattern pieces in that envelope and do not cut them up.

4 making your sample

Now that you have four finished pattern pieces with all markings and seam allowances in place, you are ready to cut out and construct your sample, or toile.

GETTING SET UP

You will need a length of mediumweight calico (see page 28). Your fabric will usually come in a width of either 115cm (45in) or 150cm (60in). Iron the calico if necessary.

Give yourself plenty of space to lay your fabric flat, whether on a large table or on the floor. Note that it is easier to pin on a hard surface than a carpeted floor.

Do keep in mind that it is rare to get a perfect fit from your first sample (toile), so do not worry if you need to make more adjustments: I will cover this in more detail a bit later on.

ARRANGING PATTERNS ON FABRIC

This arrangement is called the **layplan** (see also page 26). For your sample (toile), you will be cutting the pieces as follows:

Front Bodice: Cut × 1 (on the fold)

Back Bodice: Cut × 2 (pair)

Front Skirt: Cut × 1 (on the fold)

Back Skirt: Cut × 2 (pair)

Preparing the fabric

Fold your fabric in half: this allows you to cut two symmetrical pieces at once to create a pair. You can then also place the centre-front seam edges of your patterns exactly on the fold of the fabric.

Do not cut along the fold line. Instead, cut around all of the other edges and then, when unpinned, the fabric opens up as a symmetrical piece.

There are two ways to prepare your fabric, depending on the size of your pattern pieces. Try option 1 first and then move to option 2 if you don't have enough room. Make sure the fabric is not twisted and the fold sits nice and straight.

Option 1: Fold the fabric in half with both selvedge/selvage edges together. This works well for the smaller sizes.

Option 2: Fold the cut edge of the fabric so the selvedge edges fold back onto themselves. This works well for bigger sizes.

Tip

· When you use your chosen dress fabric, fold the right sides together (**RST**), so you are pinning onto the wrong side, to keep the right side nice and clean.

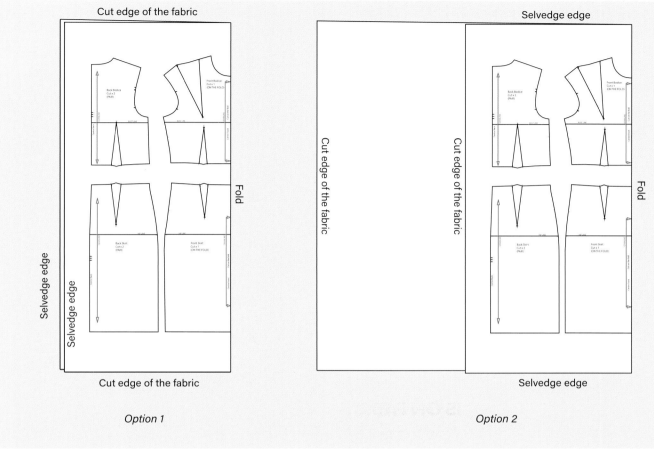

Cut edge of the fabric

Selvedge edge

Fold

Cut edge of the fabric

Option 1

Selvedge edge

Cut edge of the fabric

Cut edge of the fabric

Fold

Selvedge edge

Option 2

Positioning your patterns

Place your Front Bodice and Front Skirt patterns on the fabric first, with the centre front sitting exactly on the folded edge of the fabric.

Then, place the Back Bodice alongside the Front Bodice, and the Back Skirt alongside the Front Skirt. If they will fit onto the fabric, you can prepare to pin them, but if not, you will need to rejig your fabric as shown in the diagrams above.

Keep the pattern pieces all the same way up, as some fabrics can look different when cut at a 90-degree angle, especially satins and velvet.

Lining up grainlines

Before pinning your pattern pieces in place, make sure your grainlines sit parallel to your selvedge edge, or at 90 degrees to it. To check that your grainlines are level, use a tape measure to measure each end of the grainline from the selvedge edge.

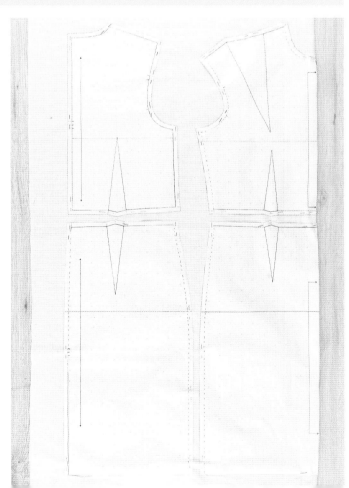

PINNING YOUR PATTERNS IN PLACE

When you are happy with the positioning, you can pin the patterns in place.

Pin within the seam allowance, in line with the pattern-piece edge.

- Do not pin with your pin going off the pattern as you do not want to cut the pin with scissors or a rotary cutter.
- Pin corners first to keep key areas in place.
- Then, pin in between to secure the whole pattern in place.
- Pin at the base of darts and important notches to keep them in place when cutting your notches.
- Place a pin exactly in the point of a dart and anchor it in place. See the illustration below and pages 64–65 where I explain this in more detail.

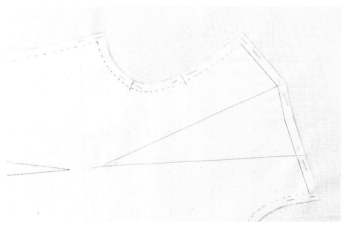

An example of a pattern piece correctly pinned.

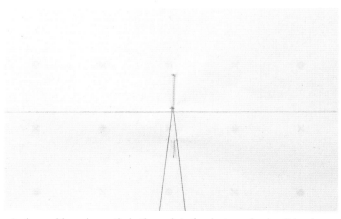

A pin positioned exactly in the point of a dart, anchoring it in place.

How to pin your patterns to the fabric

This may feel very awkward at first, but pinning does become easier and more natural.

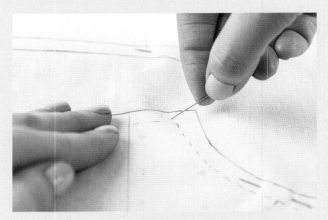

1 Hold the pin between your thumb, index finger and middle finger. Using the other hand, hold the fabric and paper pattern down firmly, with your index finger and middle finger either side of where you want to pin.

2 Point the pin at a 45-degree angle, pierce the fabric and slide the pin along briefly before tilting the pin back up and out of the fabric. Your fabric and pattern pieces should sit totally flat once pinned.

Tip

- *Do not worry about over-pinning, as long as your pattern is sitting exactly flat.*

CUTTING OUT IN CALICO

When you have everything pinned in place, you are ready to cut out your sample (toile).

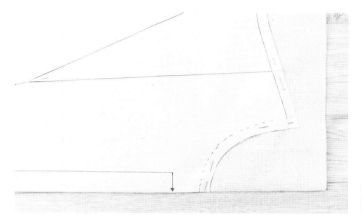

1 Make sure the centre pattern pieces sit exactly on the fold of the fabric before cutting.

2 It can help to loosely cut around each pattern piece first, to separate the pieces from each other.

3 Using a sharp pair of dressmaking scissors, cut exactly alongside the pattern-paper edge. Keep the scissors in contact with the table the whole time you cut out. Cut and then slide the scissors along. You need only use a third of the actual scissor blade to ensure more accuracy.

• Do not lift your fabric off the table. If you have pinned well you can turn your pieces, but try to keep everything as flat as possible when cutting out.

4 Use the tip of your scissors to cut around the curved areas and any corners.

Using a rotary cutter

You can use a rotary cutter with a cutting mat, but it does take some practice to get used to. Personally, I use a combination of rotary cutter for the large areas of the pattern, and scissors for the more fiddly areas, such as 'V' necklines with points and any tight curves.

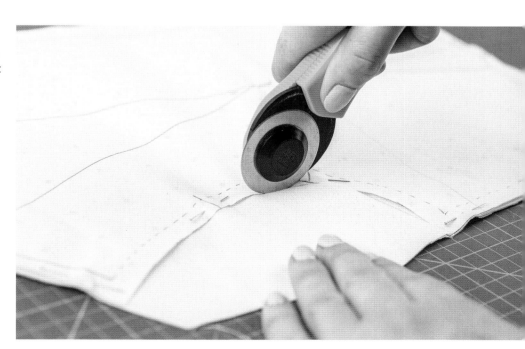

MARKING THE WRONG SIDE OF THE FABRIC

Using tailors' chalk, mark the WRONG side of the fabric with a little cross on the corner of each piece, within the seam allowance.

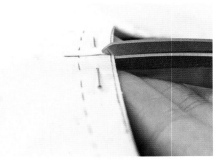

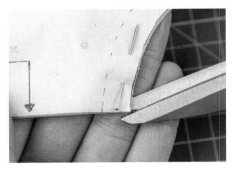

Tip

- If your fabric looks the same front and back, choose which side you think looks best and mark it, so you know when piecing your garment together.

CUTTING NOTCHES

You will need to snip notches approximately 5mm (¼in) long using the tip of your scissors. Do not cut more than this as you want this snip to be within your seam allowance. The notches are hugely important so do make sure you snip them all!

MARKING YOUR CENTRES

Where pattern pieces are pinned on the fold of the fabric, snip a notch exactly on the fold before you unpin your pattern pieces, as this will be useful when contructing your garment.

Make sure you mark the centre notch on the front neckline, front waistline on the bodice and on the skirt.

Preparing to sew your sample (toile) together

Keep your patterns pinned to your fabric until you are ready to use that particular piece.

PREPARING A DART

The Front Bodice piece is used to demonstrate the dart preparation and techniques.

- On each pattern piece where you have a dart, you will need to have notched where the ends of your dart meet the edge of the paper pattern.

- You then need to make sure you have a pin marking the tip of your dart. I like to insert a pin exactly at the tip and then anchor it onto the paper pattern by putting it back through in the middle of the dart.

- You can now take out the pins that are around the edge of the pattern but leave the one in at the tip of the dart.

- Holding the pin tightly on the underside of the fabric, lift and remove the paper pattern over the pin head, leaving the pin through the two layers of fabric.

MARKING THE TIP OF THE DART ON THE FABRIC

There are two options:

- You can mark the tip of the dart on the fabric using a fabric marker. Mark a small dot exactly where the pin is on both layers of the fabric. This is quick and easy to do.

- You could also thread a hand-sewing needle and sew two small hand-stitches exactly where the pin is, on both layers. Leave the ends long so they don't get pulled out.

PINNING YOUR DARTS

1 Lay your fabric flat on the table and find the two notches for the base of a dart.

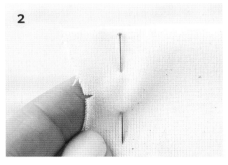

2 Place the notches directly on top of each other with the right sides of the fabric facing each other. Pin in place. This creates a fold in the fabric. It helps to always prepare your dart so the fold is sitting to the right of the notches.

3 Find the tip of the dart and pinch it so it sits on the fold of the fabric. Place a pin exactly in line with it, through both layers of the fabric. Place a few more pins along the folded dart to keep it flat. You can iron this to keep it flat and neat.

4 Using a fabric marker, draw a thin line from the notches to the tip of the dart using a ruler. This is your line to stitch onto.

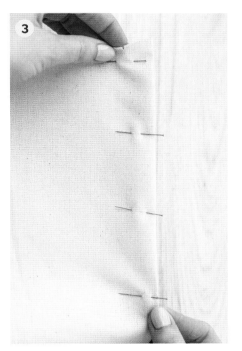

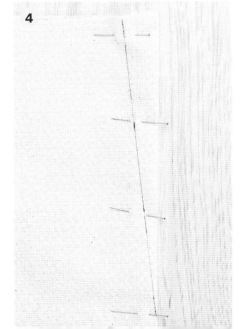

Tip

- *Make sure all of your darts are the correct way around before sewing, with the right sides pinned together.*

SEWING YOUR DARTS

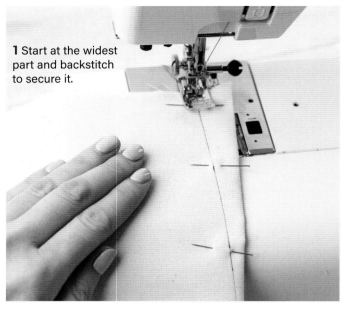

1 Start at the widest part and backstitch to secure it.

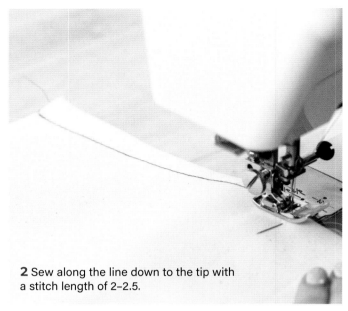

2 Sew along the line down to the tip with a stitch length of 2–2.5.

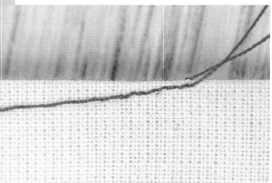

3 Just before you reach the tip, reduce your stitch length to 1, as you do not want to backstitch. Continue to sew two stitches along the very edge of the fold of the fabric to reduce having a bulky point in your dart. Run your stitching off the end of the fabric and tie the threads together.

Finished, sewn darts.
See also page 68 for an alternative method of sewing the bodice darts.

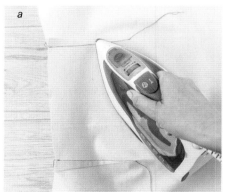

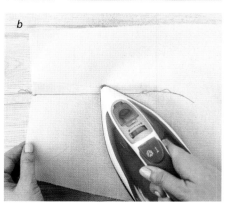

4 Once you have sewn your darts, press your front darts towards the side seams (**a**) and your back darts towards the centre (**b**).

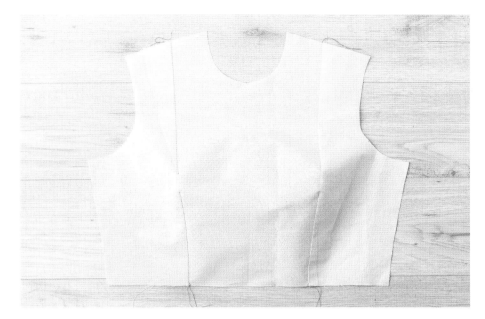

How your bust darts should look on the Front Bodice, from the right side.

Double-pointed darts

For dresses with no waistline, you will need to mark and sew a double-pointed dart, which has two tips. Transfer the markings to the wrong side of your fabric, using a fabric marker to mark the tips and middle points. Then draw the lines in and fold the dart, lining up the points and tips.

Sew a double-pointed dart as if you were sewing two separate darts. Start in the middle and backstitch, then sew to the tip before sewing a few small stitches along the edge. Then return to the middle, go over your backstitching and sew to the other tip. Remember to decrease your stitch length as you get to the tips.

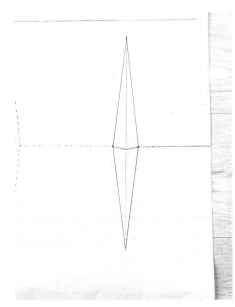

A double-pointed dart indicated on a pattern piece.

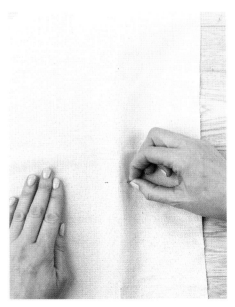

Pinning the centre of a double-pointed dart.

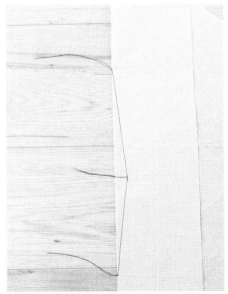

A completed double-pointed dart.

Continual dart 'cheat technique'

Sewing bust darts can be tricky at first. If you are not careful, you can get a point at the ends of the darts. However, this cheat method enables you to sew the bust darts in one go and achieve a neater finish from both the inside and the outside.

• Prepare your Front Bodice darts by pinning and drawing on the dart stitch lines.

• Start at the shoulder and sew down your dart towards the point. Don't reduce your stitch length. Instead, when you reach the point, carry on along 2mm (a scant ⅛in) from the edge of the fold towards the next point. Then carry on sewing down the dart towards the waistline.

You will find this cheat method useful when using plain fabrics for your final garment, as the normal dart will be very noticeable on the bust.

A continual dart pinned.

Continual dart on a bodice sample (toile) once sewn.

Cheat technique.

Traditional method.

Tip

• You can use carbon paper and a tracing wheel to mark the dart onto your fabric. Always test carbon paper on your fabric before using it to ensure that it will come off.

Pinning and sewing your sample (toile)

As you are not sewing on a sleeve for the sample, the construction is straightforward and reasonably quick to do.

Important note

• *This method is for making your sample only. The order of sewing changes for your final garment. See page 142.*

1 Sew all of your darts first. You will have:
   4 × darts on your Front Bodice;
   2 × darts on your Back Bodice pieces – one on each side;
   2 × darts on your Front Skirt pieces – one on each side;
   2 × darts on your Back Skirt pieces – one on each side.

2 Once sewn, press your front darts towards the side seams and your back darts towards the centre seam. Pin them in place along your seam edges. Make sure they are folded the correct way so they sit neatly on the seam edge. See the photos on the right.

Wrongly pressed dart.

Correctly pressed dart.

3 Pin and sew the Front Skirt to the Front Bodice at the waistline, right sides facing, matching up the darts and centre front. You do not need to neaten the edges of your seam allowances on your sample (toile) but remember to iron your seams open to get a neat finish and a better fitting garment. Set your iron to 2 dots (medium temperature) and use steam for a smooth finish.

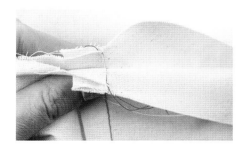

Make sure the darts line up neatly by holding in place and checking before pinning.

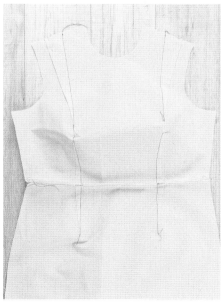

Your sample (toile) should look like this, on the inside...

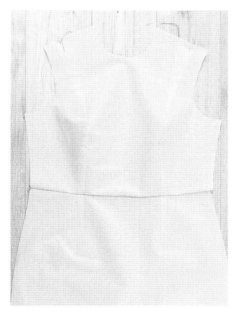

...and like this from the outside.

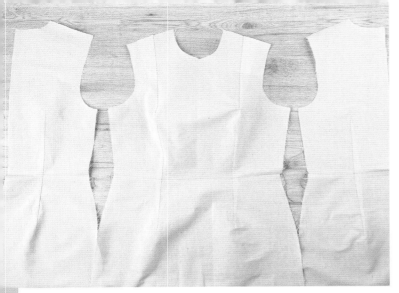

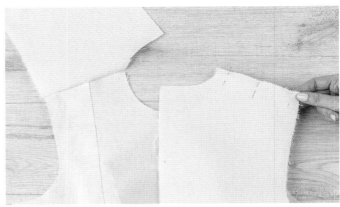

4 Pin and sew the Back Skirt pieces to the Back Bodices at the waistline, right sides facing, matching up the darts. Make sure you have a pair and not two of one side. Lay them out flat the right way around to check, as shown above.

5 Pin right sides together and sew the shoulder seams.

Lining up seams

When you line up some seams, like the shoulder seams, there will be a step and you may think the seams won't match. Just remember that the raw edges may not always be exactly the same length, but the bit that should match is the exact position of the seam allowance (**a**).

If unsure, pin the seam together where you want to sew and check that when opened out, the line runs smoothly (**b**).

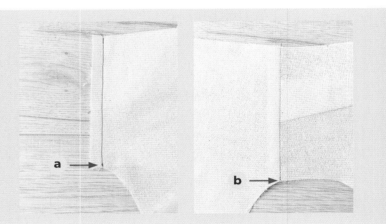

COMPLETING YOUR SAMPLE (TOILE)

You will need to leave an opening in the sample so that you can try it on. There are two different options for completing your sample (toile), depending on whether or not you have someone to help you pin the opening closed, as you won't be inserting a zip at this stage.

Option 1 has the opening in the centre-back seam.

Option 2 has the opening in a side seam.

Whichever method you choose, when sewing long sections like the side seams, always follow the steps below:

- Always place a pin at the top of the seam first and then place a pin at the bottom of the seam.

- Then look for any notches or seams and match those up before pinning in place.

- Finally, you can pin everything in between those first few key pins.

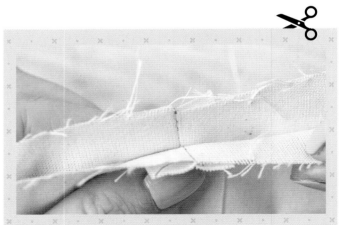

Tip

- *When matching seams up, pinch the seams in place with your fingertips. Pull open the seam allowance to see that they are lined up perfectly at the stitch line before pinning.*

Option 1 – Centre-back opening

If you have someone to help fit your sample (toile) on you, you can have the opening at the centre back as your friend can pin the centre-back seam together for you.

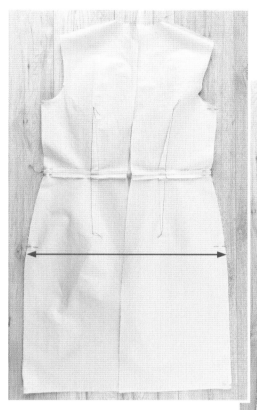

1 Pin and sew the side seams.

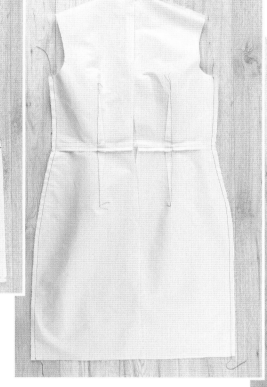

Side seams sewn together.

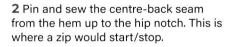

2 Pin and sew the centre-back seam from the hem up to the hip notch. This is where a zip would start/stop.

Note: Do not pin the centre back of your bodice pieces, as this stays open.

You are now ready to try on your sample (toile).

Option 2 – Side-seam opening

If you don't have anyone to help fit your sample (toile) on you, the opening should be on a side seam so that you can pin the seam together as best you can.

1 Choose on which side you want the opening to be. Pin and sew that side seam, from the hem up to the hip notch. This is where a zip would start/stop. Next, pin and sew the full length of the other side seam, from the hem to under the arm.

2 With a notch, mark 15cm (6in) below the neckline on the centre back. This will allow room for your head. Pin and sew the full length of the centre-back seam from this notch down to the hem.

You are now ready to try on your sample.

How to make this outfit ⊢

This fabulous outfit consists of a full cotton circle skirt with a waistband (see pages 128 and 156). An underskirt adds fullness and a lot of fun to the look. It is paired with a simple sleeveless top (see pages 154 and 103) with a boatneck neckline (page 97). You could make the skirt in a duchess satin and the top in crepe to turn it into a striking evening look.

5 altering your sample

You should now have your sample (toile) ready to try on.
You will need pins and a mirror. You should also have your set
of blocks to hand.

Ideally, ask someone to help fit your sample (toile) to you. If you are by yourself, just pin as best as you can. You can always gauge what needs to be altered, take it off to pin and then try it back on. It takes a little longer, but you can still do it.

To demonstrate the alterations, I am working on a mannequin, but it is more accurate to alter the dress while you are wearing it.

- Put your sample (toile) on inside out, so that the seams are all visible and accessible. This will help you to pin accurately. Pin up the opening along the stitch line depending on which seam allowance you have chosen –1cm (⅜in) or 1.5cm (⅝in).

- It is always best to have a sample (toile) that is slightly too big for you as you can sculpt it to fit you. So, don't panic if it looks a little frumpy at this point.

- Also, don't worry if your sample (toile) is too tight in a few places, as this can be altered. But, if your sample (toile) is too tight all over, I would consider tracing off the next size up. It will be worth the extra time to get it right.

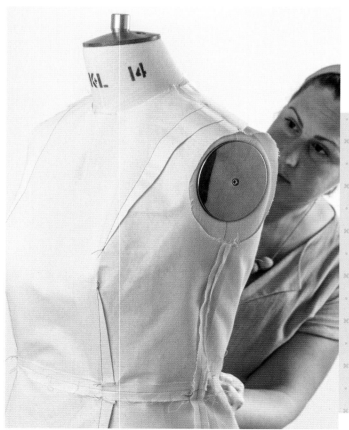

Tips for pinning your sample (toile) to fit you perfectly

- *When you pinch in any fullness, try to pin your seams evenly so that the seam line sits exactly on the fold.*

- *Try to take in the same amount on either side of the seam line you are working on.*

- *Leave your pins in place on the sample (toile) when you are finished, as these are your markers for altering your paper pattern.*

Creating a better fit

Here are six simple steps to follow to create a better fit:

1. ALTERING YOUR SIDE SEAMS

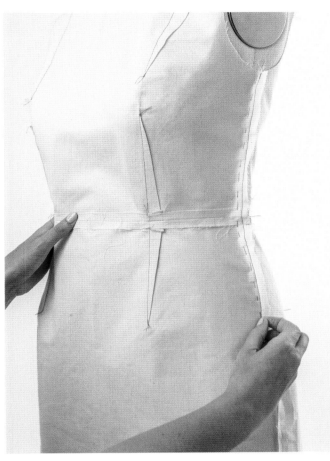

2. ALTERING YOUR SHOULDER SEAMS

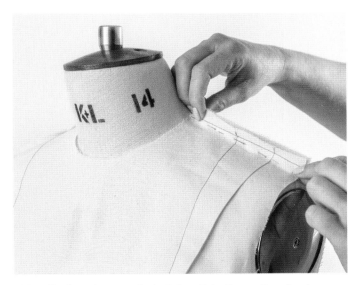

This will take in the sample (toile) across the chest, the waist and hips for a better fit.

a Lift your arm and take in the seam under the arm evenly. Drop your arm back down once pinned to check the fit. Try to alter it evenly on both sides of the body.

b Continue to take in the side seam down to the waist, hips and hem if needed. Don't make it too tight so it pulls across the body. Make sure your pins form a smooth, gradual line.

c If your sample (toile) is too tight, open your side seam where it is pulling and try it back on. Measure the gaps and make a note of it on your sample (toile), for example, 'add 2cm (¾in) into seam.'

This will allow the sample (toile) to fit better on the chest and bust.

a Lift the shoulder seam and pin the front and back seams evenly as shown.

b None of us are symmetrical, but unless you have an obvious difference in both shoulders, use the same alteration for both shoulders.

c If you do have one shoulder lower than the other, alter them accordingly and make sure you work on your pattern as a full front piece. Draw around the bodice, and then mirror it on the paper so you are working onto a 'left' and 'right' side – remember that you had your dress on inside out.

3. MARKING THE SHOULDER POINT

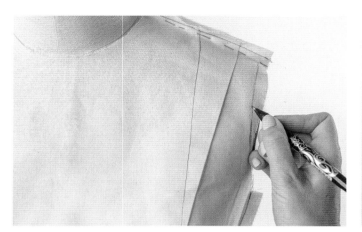

This is where your sleeve, or seam edge will sit on your shoulder.

a Look closely at your shoulder to see where you would want a sleeve, or seam edge for a sleeveless dress, to sit.

b Mark with a fabric pen.

5. ALTERING THE WAISTLINE

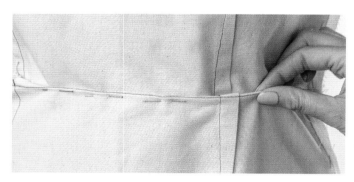

This will allow you to lift the waistline, if needed. Note that you do not want to alter the skirt pattern. Instead, you are lifting up the skirt waistline seam to sit higher on the bodice. You will then alter the bodice pattern to create a higher waistline.

a Pinch the waistline seam and lift it up to where you want it to sit. Make sure the waistline is level front and back. Pin in place. This is tricky to pin so take your time.

b If you are unsure where the waistline should sit, close your eyes and put your hands on your waist. This is usually where the waistline should be.

c If you need to extend your waistline, you will need to go back to page 53 to lengthen the bodice pattern.

4. ALTERING THE CENTRE FRONT

This will allow you to take in any excess from the neckline.

a If you have bagginess across your neckline, pinch in the fullness at the centre of the neckline and pin. Continue pinning down towards the bust. Try not to take anything off the centre front at the waistline.

b If you have excess at the centre front on the waistline, try taking that in using the side seams instead – you don't want to interfere with the waistline.

c If you still need to take in from the centre front, make sure you continue taking in the skirt also, as these pieces need to match at the waistline.

6. ALTERING AND PINNING THE OPENING SEAM

a When you pin the centre-back opening, (or side-seam opening) closed, draw a line exactly where the pins sit before removing them, so you know where the new stitch line is.

b If you need to take off excess from the centre-back opening, keep it equal on both sides of the seam. If you take off excess from a side opening, make sure the alteration is the same on the other side seam.

c When you have finished altering and pinning your sample (toile), take a photo from the front, side and back, so you can look at yourself with fresh eyes.

These six simple alterations will be sufficient to help you create a well-fitting dress. If you still have some fit issues, there are a few extra steps to follow once you have transferred your alterations to your pattern pieces.

Transferring your alterations to the paper pattern

If you traced off the blocks with no amendments, you can work straight onto those patterns. However, if you made any alterations, always trace off a new set of blocks to work on, so you can always go back to the original set if you make a mistake.

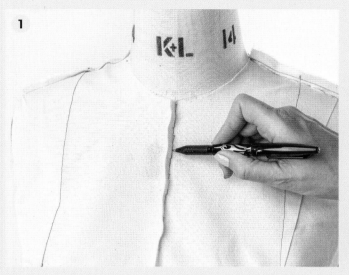

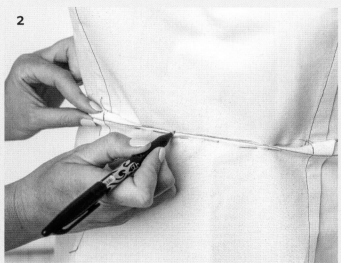

1 To transfer the alterations from the sample (toile) to the paper pattern, you will need to mark the alterations on the sample (toile) itself.

The pin line is your new stitching line: using a pencil or pen, draw directly on the pin line on both sides of where you have pinned.

2 For the waistline, you only need to draw onto the bodice where the fold line sits.

3 Once you have drawn on your new stitching line, you can take the pins out.

4 You can now start to transfer the alterations onto your bodice and skirt patterns.

Transferring your new marks

On each seam you have altered, you will need to copy the new stitch lines onto the paper pattern. You can either lay the pattern directly on top of the sample to copy, or you can use a tape measure to mark the adjustments accurately onto the pattern.

Transfer your alteration markings from the sample onto the paper pattern in pencil first.

ALTERING YOUR SHOULDER SEAMS

Start simple with the shoulder alterations (see overleaf). Pin the Front Bodice dart closed on the pattern piece to lay it flat. Draw the new stitch line in red pen.

1 The shoulder seam lines should remain straight. Take the same amount off the front and back shoulder seams.

2 Draw in a new seam allowance 1cm (⅜in) from the red line. Any excess is marked in blue dashes and then cut off the pattern piece.

Mark your shoulder point

If you altered your shoulder line, draw the new stitch line on your pattern piece. Keeping the gentle curve, graduate down to meet the original armhole stitch line. Draw a new seam allowance and cut off any excess.

ALTERING THE CENTRE FRONT

When you remove the pins on the centre-front alteration, you will have drawn a 'V' on your sample. However, the centre-front pattern is cut on the fold, so only mark half of the width of the measurement on the centre-front neckline. Then, draw a straight line down to meet the original centre-front seam edge at the waistline.

As this pattern piece will be cut on the fold, the line must be straight and no seam allowance is needed. Just cut off the excess.

Sample with shoulder, armhole and centre-front alterations lines drawn on.

Pattern piece with new stitch lines drawn in red pen. A new seam allowance is drawn in and the excess marked in blue ready to be cut off.

Excess is cut off. Pattern alteration is complete.

ALTERING YOUR SIDE SEAMS

Pin the pattern pieces together at the waist seam so the stitch lines sit directly on top of each other.

• It is difficult to pin exactly the same on each side of the body, so go with the average of the two seams. Mark your new stitch line in red, making sure you take the same off the front and back pattern pieces.

• Make sure the new seam is straight on the bodice side seam and has a smooth curve at the waistline and hip line, following the natural curve of the body.

Pattern pieces with new stitch lines drawn in red pen.

A new seam allowance is drawn in and excess is cut off. Side seam alteration is complete.

ALTERING THE WAISTLINE

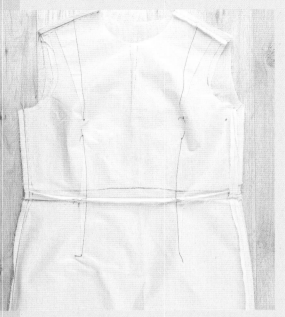

You may find that the alteration line of the waistline is a bit uneven when unpinned. Just level it out as best as you can, mirroring the opposite side.

1 Pin the waist dart closed. Then, place your bodice pattern piece onto the seam and draw in your new stitch line in red pen.

2 Join the Front and Back Bodice patterns at the side seam with a pin, making sure the stitch lines sit exactly on top of each other. When drawing your new stitch line, make sure the waistline is a smooth continuous line.

3 Draw in your new seam allowance and mark the excess ready to cut off.

The completed alteration with the excess cut off.

ALLOWING FOR A ZIP OPENING

Whether your zip will be in the centre back or the side seam, make sure you have a 1.5cm (⅝in) seam allowance to allow for your zip. You can reduce the seam allowance to exactly 1cm (⅜in) for a concealed zip, once you perfect the fit. Your pattern alteration is complete.

How to make this dress ⊢
This simple yet classic straight dress is made in a casual denim fabric. It consists of a fitted skirt (see page 122), a boatneck neckline (page 97) and no sleeves (page 103). The simple cut allows for some fun accessorizing with belts and jewellery. You could make it in a printed polycotton fabric to create a vibrant, stylish outfit.

Choosing the correct size sleeve

Once you have perfected the fit of your sample (toile) and made any alterations, you can work out which sleeve block you need to trace off to create your sleeves.

- Measure the full armhole using the Front and Back Bodice pattern pieces. Make sure you measure the stitch line without seam allowance, with the tape measure on its side.

- Your sleeve pattern needs to be at least 2cm (¾in) longer than the armhole measurement, as this will add sufficient ease into the sleeve head.

- The armhole measurements for the sleeve nests are listed below, to help you choose the correct size.

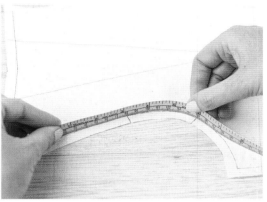

Measuring the armhole.

When you have your sleeve pattern traced off, measure around your bicep loosely. Next, measure across your sleeve pattern at the widest part, from each underarm seam. This is your bicep measurement.

If you find that the sleeve is too narrow, you can add fullness into the upper arm by doing a **bicep alteration** (see opposite).

Size	Armhole Measurement	
	(cm)	**(in)**
1	40	15¾
2	42	16½
3	44	17¼
4	46	18⅛
5	48	18⅞
6	50	19⅝
7	52	20½
8	54.5	21½
9	56.5	22¼
10	58.5	23
11	60.5	23¾
12	63.5	25
13	66	26
14	68.5	27
15	71	28
16	73.5	29
17	76	30
18	78.5	30⅞
19	81	31⅞

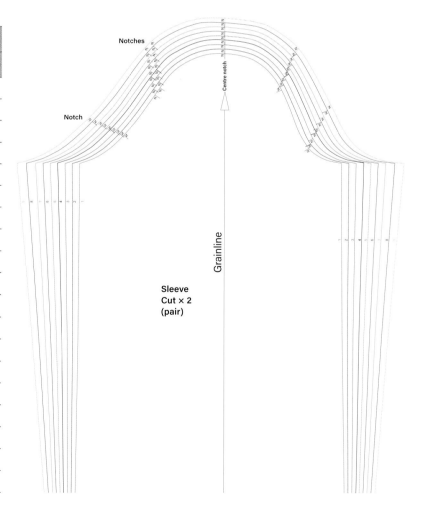

BICEP ALTERATION

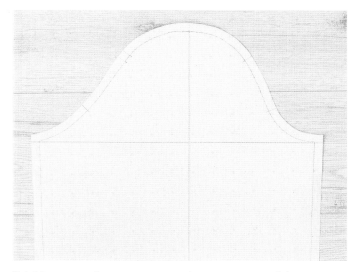

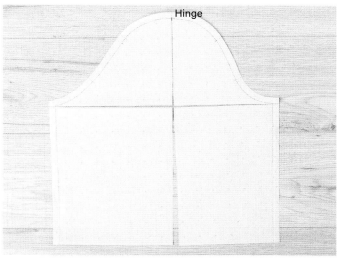

1 Add a seam allowance to your sleeve pattern and then cut it out.

2 Draw a horizontal line across your sleeve pattern, at the fullest part, where the underarm and sleeve-head seam allowances meet. This is your bicep measurement.

3 Draw a line vertically from the centre sleeve-head notch.

4 Cut up the vertical line but stop exactly at the seam allowance to create a hinge.

5 Now, snip into the seam allowance from the top of the line but keep the pattern pieces joined. This allows you to open up the sleeve without altering the seam line.

6 Next, cut across the horizontal lines, again stopping at the seam allowance on each side, to create a hinge.

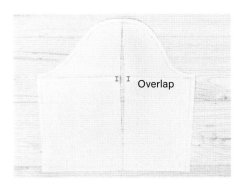

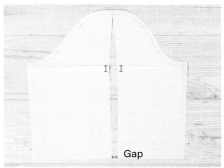

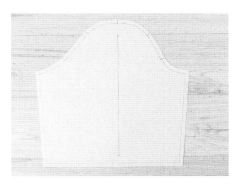

7 Overlap pieces at the bicep line. This allows you to open out the sleeve to create the extra fullness needed. Adjust to your bicep measurement.

8 Rejoin the seam at the hem, unless you want to add a little bit extra into the hem of the sleeve.

9 Redraw the sleeve head and hem if needed. Trace off your new pattern piece.

Checking your pattern before cutting out

It is worth making a new sample (toile) in calico to check that the alterations you have made are correct.

Before you do this, however, it is important to check that your seams all match where they will be sewn together. Make sure you close your darts before pinning your seams together.

Use the following checklist:

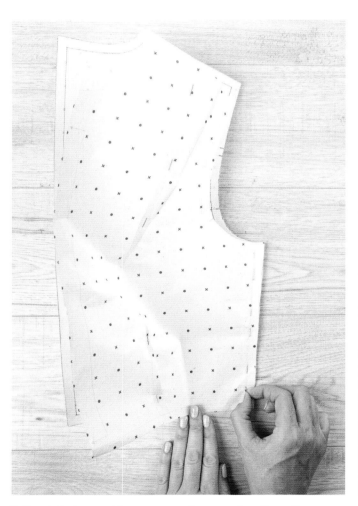

1 Check that your side seams are the same length on the bodice patterns.

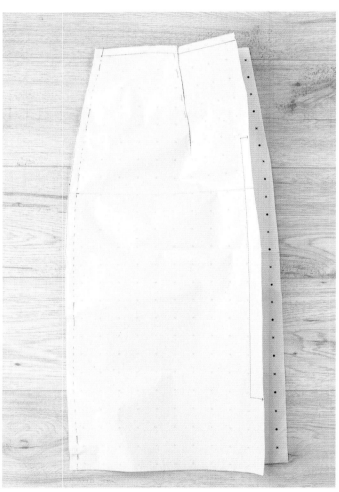

2 Check that your side seams are the same length on the skirt patterns.

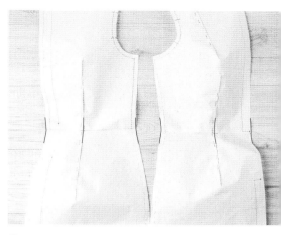

3 Check that your waistlines join up neatly and the lines flow, by joining the side seams.

4 Check that your hemline joins up neatly and the line flows, by joining the side seams.

5 Check that the bodice waist matches your skirt waist on both the front and back pieces. Also, check your darts line up perfectly at the waistline.

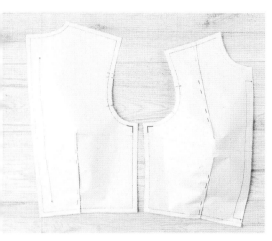

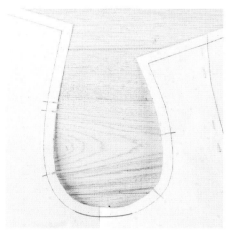

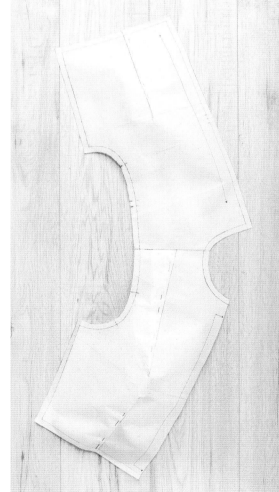

6 Check the armhole seams are near to right angles for a neat seam finish.

7 Join the bodice side seams to check the curve of the armhole.

8 Check your back and front shoulder seams are the same length.

9 Join your shoulder seams together and check that the armhole flows, as well as the neckline.

Advanced pattern alterations

If you still have a few fit issues, you can consider the following alterations to the patterns, but please only do them if you have the confidence to try them.

GAPING ARMHOLE

Even after altering the side seams and shoulder seams, the armhole can sometimes gape on the front. If you are planning to attach a sleeve, don't panic as this gaping is a good thing – it adds wearing ease to the armhole.

However, if you are not planning to add a sleeve, the gaping should be addressed.

Pinch the fabric where it is gaping on the armhole seam and put a pin in to secure it. Measure how much you need to take out. You will move that extra volume into the shoulder dart with a simple technique.

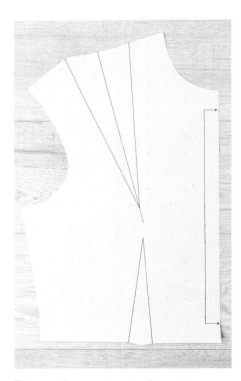

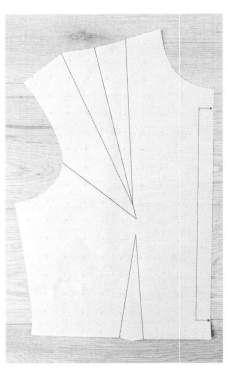

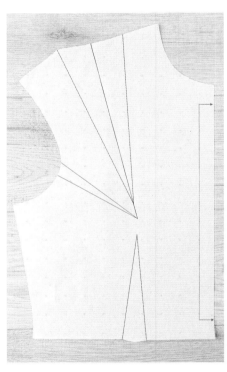

1 Trace off your Front Bodice pattern without seam allowance and cut around it.

2 Draw a line down the centre of the bust dart and extend that line by 2cm (¾in) so it meets the actual bust point. Then cut along that exact line to meet the bust point.

3 Mark on the pattern where the armhole is gaping and draw a straight line to meet the bust point.

4 Measure the amount you want to take out of the armhole and make a mark further along from the first line. Then draw another straight line from the mark to the bust point. You will have drawn a narrow dart.

5 Close the narrow dart, which in turn will open the shoulder dart. The fullness has now moved into your shoulder dart!

6 Redraw your shoulder dart so it stops 2cm (¾in) from the bust point, otherwise, you will have a point right on your bust when you sew your dart.

7 Redraw the armhole shape so it is a smooth curve, then add your seam allowances.

How to make this outfit
This knee-length A-line skirt, with box pleats (see page 132), is fabulous in a cotton print. It is paired with a simple T-shirt style cotton top (page 154), with a curved neckline (page 94) and capped sleeves (page 110). Making the skirt in a heavy denim would allow it to really hold its shape. Mixing the denim with a printed cotton top would be truly striking.

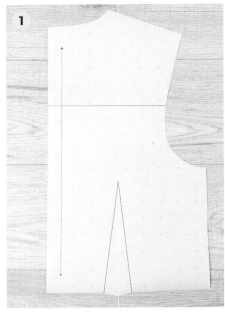

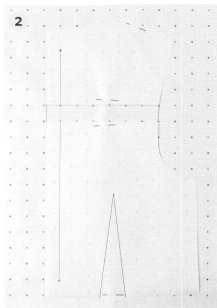

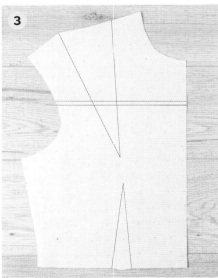

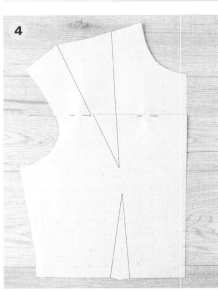

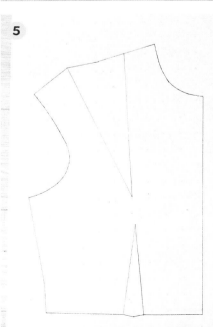

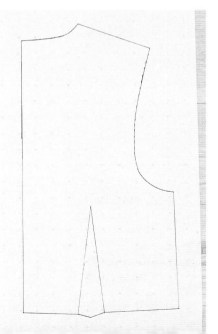

ROUNDED BACK

If you have a rounded back, you may need to add into the Back Bodice pattern for a better fit. The alteration will prevent the garment from drawing up in the front and falling towards the back.

1 Draw around your Back Bodice pattern without seam allowance and cut out. Draw a horizontal line across the pattern at the centre of the armhole.

2 Cut along this line, separating the bodice into two pieces. Put a new piece of paper underneath and spread the patterns out by 1.2cm (½in) or more. Redraw the armhole and centre-back seam.

3 Draw around your Front Bodice pattern. Draw a horizontal line across the front at the centre of the armhole. Fold up 6mm (¼in).

4 Redraw your darts to ensure that they line up. Also redraw your armhole.

5 Retrace both Front and Back Bodice pattern pieces and add seam allowances.

FULL-BUST ALTERATION (FBA)

Your sample should be a good fit if you have worked with the correct measurements according to your bust. However, if your bust is curvaceous, it can cause real problems with the fit. This alteration will make the bodice front wider and longer to accommodate a fuller bust.

Firstly, you must move your shoulder dart to the side seam.

 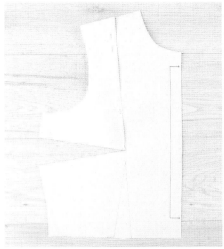

1 Trace around your Front Bodice without seam allowance.

2 Draw a line down the centre of the shoulder dart and extend that line by 2cm (¾in) so it meets the actual bust point.

3 Draw a straight line from the side seam to the bust point. Then cut along that exact line to meet the bust point.

4 Close the shoulder dart and pin in place. Your shoulder dart will now have moved to become a side dart.

Making the alteration

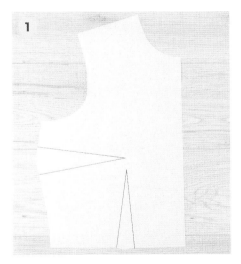 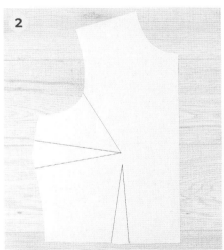 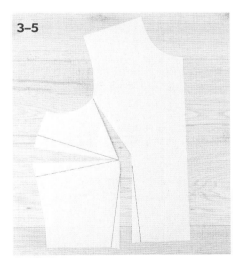

1 Retrace your Front Bodice with your new dart positions. Cut out your new pattern piece without seam allowances.

2 Draw a straight line from the bust point to the armhole.

3 Cut up the centre of the waist dart to the bust point and continue along to the armhole, keeping the armhole attached by a few millimetres.

4 Cut up the centre of the side dart to the bust point, but again, keep the pattern attached at the bust point.

5 Rearrange the cut-up pieces of your Front Bodice to add fullness at the bust point as in the photo, depending on how much you need to add. Start with 1.25cm (½in).

When opening the side dart, keep the pattern pieces parallel at the waist dart.

6 Just below the original point of the waist dart, cut along horizontally to the centre front and move the piece down so the waistlines line up.

7 Tape everything in place and trace off your new Front Bodice. Then add seam allowances. Make sure the points of your new darts start 2cm (¾in) away from the bust point for a smooth finish.

Now that you have completed the relevant alterations, you should have a sample (toile) that fits you comfortably. The next stage of the book shows you how to create a range of necklines, sleeves and skirts to help you produce your unique range of dresses.

I would recommend making your first dress in calico so that you can perfect the proportions of the added features. Once your pattern is the right fit, and you have added the features you like, you can then make lots of versions of that dress in different fabrics.

I will continue to demonstrate in calico for consistency and clarity. You can work in your final fabric choice if you feel confident with the features you are adding.

How to make this outfit
This denim pencil skirt (see page 122) is easy to make and versatile to wear. Here, it is matched with a printed cotton top (page 154), with a boatneck neckline (page 97) and no sleeves (see page 103). The loose-fitting top allows for a relaxed, comfortable look. You could make the skirt in a heavy wool for a more formal look and match it with a top in printed crepe.

MAKING THE DRESS YOUR OWN

6 adapting the pattern

Now that you have a well-fitting sample (toile), you can adapt the pattern to make it personal to you. You will be able to choose from four necklines, four sleeves and five skirts, to suit your own style.

necklines

A neckline can completely change the whole look of a dress. I recommend that you use your favourite neckline on an existing garment as a guide to help you determine the proportions and shaping. Necklines are the best place to start when adapting your pattern.

The next few pages will talk you through creating the following necklines: **curved, 'V' neckline, sweetheart and boatneck.**

Curved neckline
See page 94

'V' neckline
See page 95

Sweetheart neckline
See page 96

Boatneck neckline
See page 97

1 Whichever neckline you wish to make, first put your sample (toile) on a mannequin if you have one, or try it back on yourself. Using a measuring tape and a fabric pen, mark how low you want your neckline to sit.

2 Draw in your chosen neckline (see the following pages) and mark where on the shoulders it should sit. Try not to go too close to the dart line at this beginners' stage (with the exception of the boatneck for which you draw over the darts).

3 Draw in the back neck. Always make sure the design line is at 90 degrees to the centre-back seam, as it is easier to insert a fastening when the seams are neat right-angles.

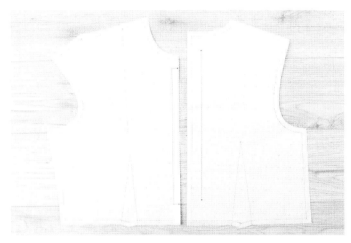

4 For every new neckline you create, trace off the Front and Back Bodice patterns with seam allowances, so you have new patterns to work from. Don't cut up your well-fitting block!

5 Fold your front shoulder dart closed and pin in place.

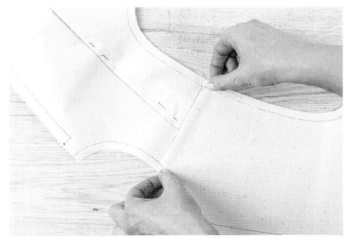

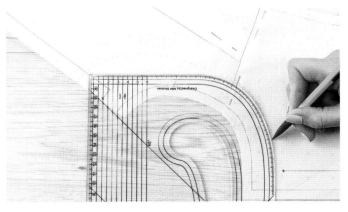

6 Pin the shoulders together along the stitch lines as if it is sewn together.

7 Place your patterns on a flat surface and get your pattern master and pencil ready.

Each of the four necklines starts at this point, with your pattern pieces pinned together at the shoulder seam.

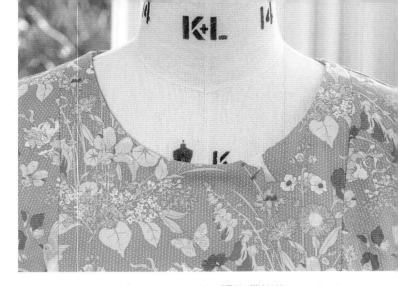

CURVED NECKLINE

Follow steps 1–7 on pages 92–93 first. Then proceed with the steps below.

1 Referring to the lines you drew on your sample (toile) in step 2, page 93, draw a smooth continuous line from the centre front, around and over the shoulder, and round to the centre back.

2 Make sure the design line is at a 90-degree angle to both the centre-front fold line and the centre-back seam.

The following three steps are repeated on every neckline:

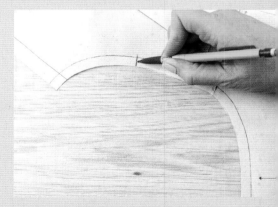

3 Add a 1cm (⅜in) seam allowance.

4 Cut off the excess pattern paper.

5 Draw a notch halfway along the curve of the front neck, between the shoulder seam and the centre front. This will help you match the neckline to your facings. You can do this on the back also, if you have lowered the back neckline. Then create your facing patterns. See page 98 for more information on facings.

'V' NECKLINE

Follow steps 1–7 on pages 92–93 first. Then proceed with the steps below.

1 Refer to the lines you drew on your sample (toile) in step 2, page 93, to mark how low you want your 'V' to go. Draw a gentle curve from the bottom of the 'V' up and over the shoulder, and round to the centre back.

2 Make sure the design line is at a 90-degree angle to the centre-back seam.

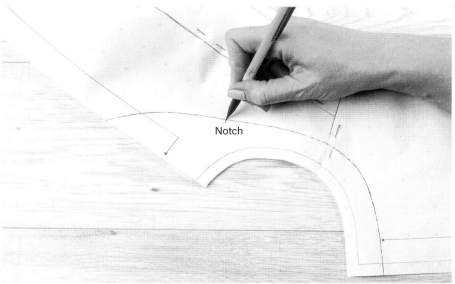

Notch

3 Draw a notch halfway along the curve of the front neck, between the shoulder seam and the centre front. This will help you match the neckline to your facings. You can do this on the back also, if you have lowered the back neckline.

4 Add a 1cm (⅜in) seam allowance. Cut off the excess pattern paper. Then create your facing patterns (see page 98).

SWEETHEART NECKLINE

Follow steps 1–7 on pages 92–93 first. Then proceed with the steps below.

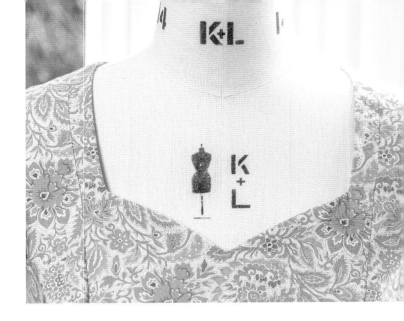

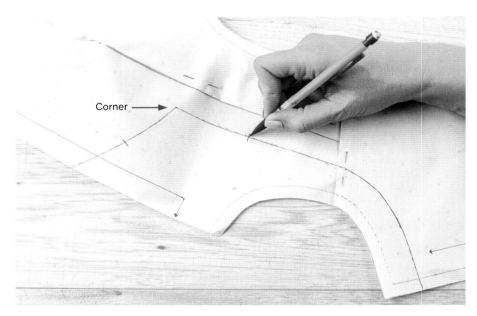

Corner

1 Refer to the lines you drew on your toile in step 2, page 93.

2 Measure where you want your 'V' to sit on the centre front. Then mark where you want the corner to be.

3 Draw a curve from the bottom of the 'V' over to the corner. Then continue the line straight up to the shoulder. I kept the line parallel with the dart.

4 Continue the line over the shoulder and then round to the centre back.

5 Make sure the design line is at a 90-degree angle to the centre-back seam.

6 Draw a notch halfway along the new curve, and also on the line from the curve to the shoulder, to help match up your neckline to your facings.

7 Add a 1cm (⅜in) seam allowance. Cut off the excess pattern paper. Then create your facing patterns. See page 98 for more information on facings.

BOATNECK NECKLINE

Follow steps 1–7 on pages 92–93 first. Then proceed with the steps below.

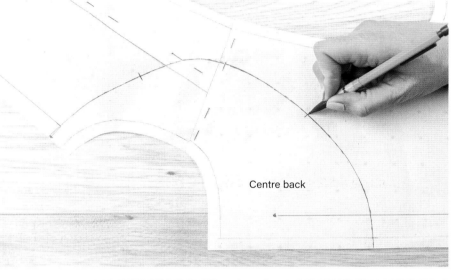

Centre back

1 Refer to the lines you drew on your toile in step 2, page 93 to mark where you want the neckline to sit on the front and shoulder.

2 Make sure the design line is at a 90 degree angle to both the centre-front fold line and the centre-back seam.

3 Draw a very gentle curve from the centre front to the shoulder. Continue it over the shoulder and round to the centre back.

4 Draw a notch halfway along the curve on the front and back, to help match up your neckline to your facings.

5 Add 1cm (⅜in) seam allowance and cut off the excess pattern paper. Then create your facing patterns. See page 98 for more information on facings.

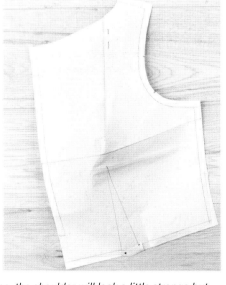

When you unpin the boatneck front pattern piece, the shoulder will look a little strange but as long as your dart has been pinned towards the side seam, it is exactly right.

Facings for necklines

A neck facing is a mirror image of your neckline that sits inside your garment. It is made using the same fabric as your garment but also has a layer of interfacing ironed to the back, to give extra support (see page 10). Sewing a facing onto a neckline hides the raw seams and holds the shape of the neckline. Facings tend to be about 4–6cm (1½–2⅜in) wide, including a seam allowance.

A finished facing on the inside of a dress (front).

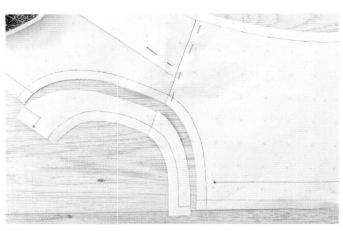

1 You will draw your facing design lines onto the same Front and Back Bodice pattern pieces that you created your neckline on. Once you have drawn in your neckline design, added seam allowance, removed the excess and marked your notches, you are ready to draw in your facing lines.

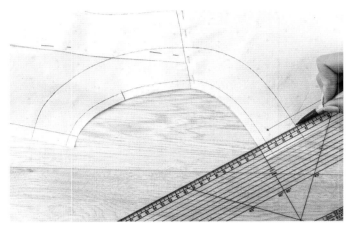

2 Draw in your facing line, between 4cm (1½in) and 6cm (2⅜in) in from the edge of your seam allowance on the neckline. The facing line should be parallel to the neckline.

Make sure the curves are smooth and the design line is at a 90-degree angle to the centre back.

3 Unpin your shoulder seams but keep the dart pinned in place. Open out your shoulder seam allowances if they were pinned back.

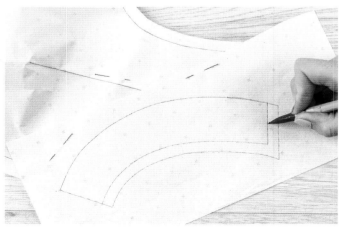

4 Place some paper over your Front Bodice pattern and trace off the new facing line along with the edge of the seam allowances on the shoulder, neckline and centre front.

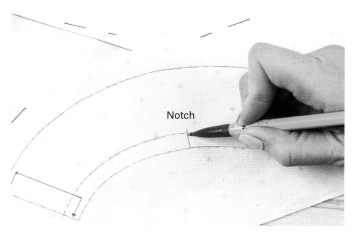

5 Mark in any notches.

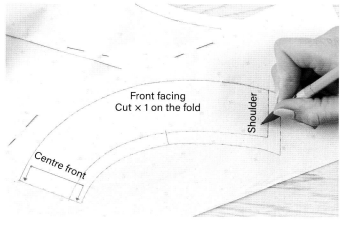

Front facing
Cut × 1 on the fold

Shoulder

Centre front

6 Label the pattern piece, including the name, size, shoulder seam and the centre front.

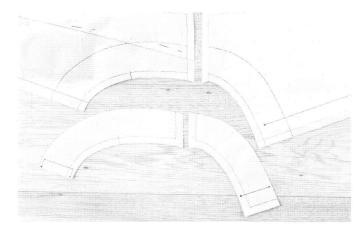

7 Repeat for the back facing. Cut out both facing pattern pieces.

PREPARING YOUR FACINGS

You will cut your facings separately from the rest of the garment once you **block fuse** the fabric (see overleaf for information on block fusing).

1 Cut a piece of fabric big enough to accommodate two of each facing.

2 Fold the fabric in half so you will cut through two layers.

3 Position your facings on the fabric to check that they fit. Make sure that the centre front is positioned on the fold.

4 Line up the grainlines.

Do not pin or cut out your facings yet.

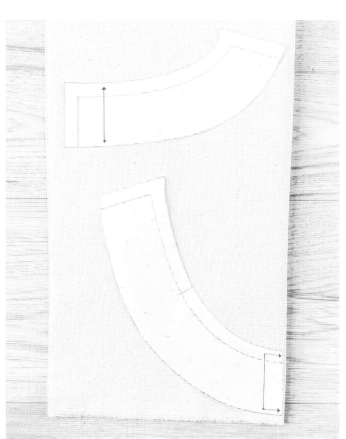

Block fusing your fabric

Block fusing is when you attach interfacing (see page 10) to the fabric before you cut out your pieces. It allows for a neater finish compared to when you cut fabric and interfacing pieces separately and then try to fuse them together. They are never exactly the same and your edges can fray.

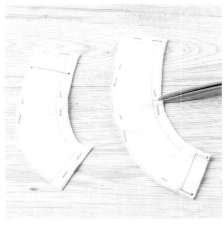

Take off the pattern pieces and open out the fabric. Cut a piece of iron-on mediumweight interfacing, slightly smaller than the fabric. Place on the fabric with the glue side facing the wrong side of the fabric. The glue side is usually either rough to the touch or shiny. Iron on the interfacing on 2 dots (medium) temperature and no steam. See the manufacturer's instructions.

Cutting and joining your facings

1 Refold your fabric, pin on your facing patterns and cut out. Snip notches, including one on the centre-front fold.

Iron the back of the facings again to make sure the interfacing is properly fused on.

2 Lay out the facing pieces, matching up the shoulder seams. Make sure the same sides of the fabric are facing up.

3 Pin the shoulder seams together, right sides facing, and sew a 1cm (⅜in) seam allowance. Press the seams open. Neaten the outside curved edge of the facing using zigzag stitch or an overlocker (serger) if you have one.

ATTACHING THE FACINGS TO THE NECKLINE

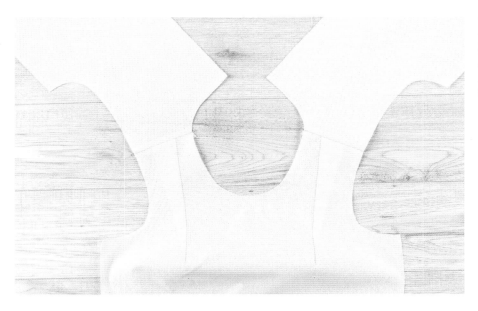

1 On the bodice, sew the darts. Then pin the shoulder seams together, right sides facing, and sew a 1cm (⅜in) seam allowance. Press the seams open, then lay the bodice flat with the right sides facing up.

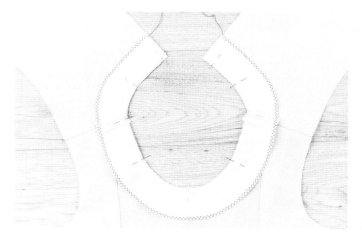 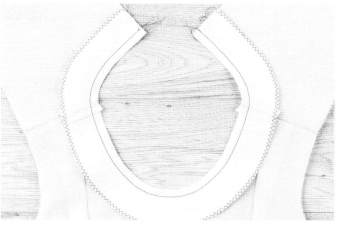

2 Position the joined facings onto the bodice with the right sides together (**RST**). Pin the centre backs first, then the shoulder seams, then match the notches on the front. Then pin in between.

3 Draw in the seam allowance on tight curves or corners to help stitch them accurately.

4 Sew a 1cm (⅜in) seam allowance all the way around, pivoting at corners if you have any.

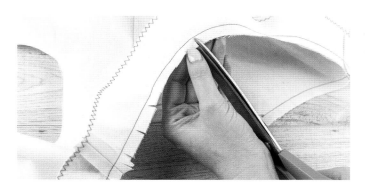

5 Snip into any curves or corners in the seam allowance. Snip to within 2mm (⅛in) of the row of stitching, being careful not to snip the stitching itself. Don't iron yet!

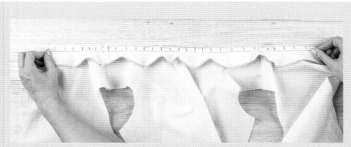 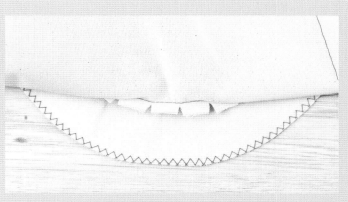

You know when you have snipped a curved seam well, as you should be able to open it out to a straight line.

The snips in the curved seam do an important job of letting your curved seam allowance spread evenly within the seam.

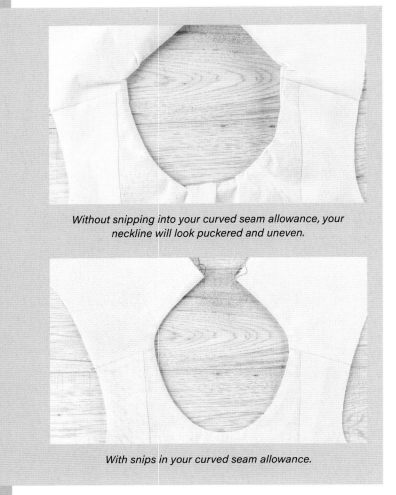

*Without snipping into your curved seam allowance, your
neckline will look puckered and uneven.*

With snips in your curved seam allowance.

A finished facing on the inside of a dress (back).

UNDERSTITCHING

This is my favourite technique as understitching gives such a
neat finish on necklines and armholes without much effort.

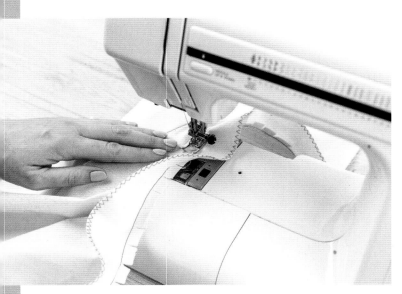

1 Start at the centre back. With the right side of the bodice
facing up, pull the facing, and both layers of seam allowance to
the right of the neckline seam.

2 Keeping your layers flat and taut, place them under the
sewing-machine foot.

3 You are going to sew through the facing and both layers of
seam allowance. You do not sew on the bodice.

4 Sew a few millimetres to the right of the neckline seam, on
the facing.

5 As you sew, keep checking underneath to make sure the
snipped seam allowance is still going to the right and not
slipping over to the left.

When you are finished, the facing and seam allowances will
roll towards the inside of the neckline. This stops the facing
popping up on the front of the garment.

Iron around the neckline from the inside, to smooth it into
position, creating a super-neat finish from the front.

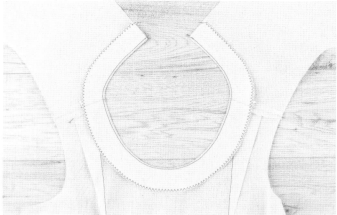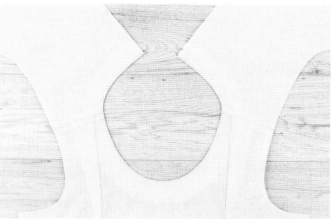

The understitching from the wrong side...

...and the right side of the sample (toile).

FOR A DRESS WITHOUT SLEEVES...

If you choose not to have sleeves on your dress or top, for a neat finish, you should draft facings for the armholes. You create them in the same way you create facings for the necklines (see pages 98–102).

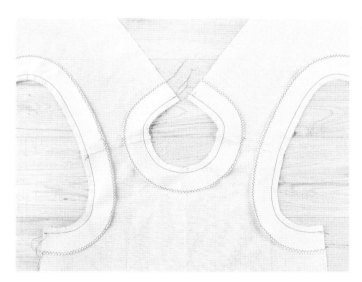

1 Draft a front armhole facing and a back armhole facing. Sew them together at the shoulder. Then, pin them onto the armhole and sew in place.

2 Snip the curved seam allowances and then understitch for a neat finish.

Tip

· *Inside your garment, tack (baste) your finished facings to the shoulder seam allowance, so they don't move.*

sleeves

A sleeve is an integral part of a dress. Sleeves for some people are functional and for others they are a fashion statement. A sleeve can totally change the style of the dress through its shape, size and flare.

The straight sleeve block is purely a starting point for adapting your sleeve to your desired style. A straight sleeve in a non stretchy fabric will restrict your movement, so adapting the sleeve to a looser fit and style will give you more room to move.

Adding fullness into the sleeve head allows for a comfortable fit and makes it easier to sew onto the bodice, therefore each sleeve in my book has gathering at the sleeve head.

Flared sleeve
See page 108

Capped sleeve
See page 110

Puff sleeve
See page 113

Butterfly sleeve
See page 116

HOW TO PREPARE AND SEW IN A SLEEVE

Gathering the sleeve head

Before you do anything with your sleeves, you need to sew two rows of gathering stitch on each sleeve head to help the sleeve head fit into the armhole.

The extra fullness you are gathering is 'ease' to make the sleeve fit comfortably, and ensure that it will not be too tight. Gathering looks like train tracks, with two rows of long stitching running parallel to each other.

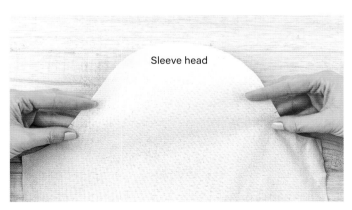

Sleeve head

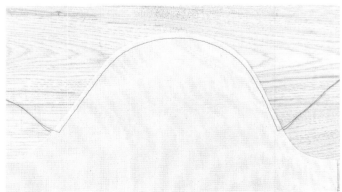

1 With the sleeve laid flat, find the two single notches nearest each edge of the sleeve.

2 Increase your stitch length to the longest setting. Pull your threads nice and long from the back of the machine. **Do not backstitch at the start or end.**

3 Starting at a notch, put your needle in the middle position and keep the edge of the fabric alongside the edge of your foot whilst you gently sew around the curve. The stitching should be about 5mm (¼in) from the edge of the fabric. Pivot as you need until you reach the other notch. Pull out the fabric from the machine and leave the threads long when cutting.

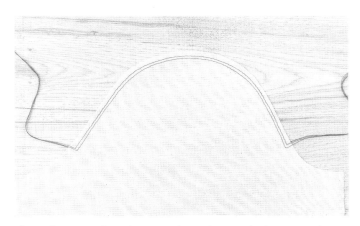

4 For the second row, start and stop in exactly the same place. For a 1cm (⅜in) seam allowance, sew 1.25cm (½in) from the edge; for a 1.5cm (⅝in) seam allowance, sew 1cm (⅜in) from the edge. Don't stitch over your gathering rows as the gathering thread becomes harder to remove. Leave the threads long again at each end.

SEWING THE SLEEVE IN PLACE

The method of sewing the sleeve in place is exactly the same for whichever style you choose.

The front and the back armholes are shaped differently. The double notches on the bodice armhole and the sleeve signify the back. You do not want to sew them on the wrong way around.

Keep all pins at a 90 degree angle to the seam allowance. Do not try to pin with them parallel to the edge of the fabric as you are pinning a curve which will make it very tricky.

Keep the pin heads visible so you pull them out just before you sew over them.

1 Your Front Bodice and Back Bodice will already be sewn together at the shoulder seams after completing the neckline.

2 Sew your gathering rows on the sleeve head.

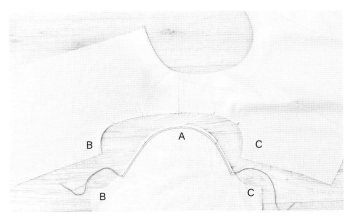

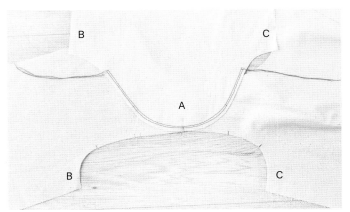

3 Lay your bodice flat on the table with the right sides facing you. Then lay the sleeves flat on the table, making sure the single and double notches match.

4 Pin one sleeve at a time. Place the pieces right sides together (**RST**) and pin the centre sleeve notch to the shoulder seam at point A.

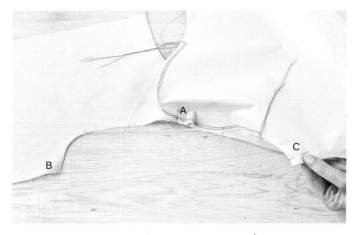

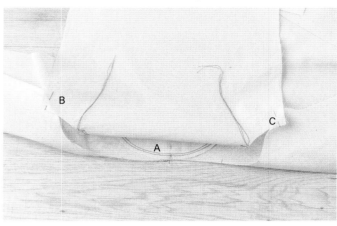

5 Next, match and pin point C of the sleeve armhole to point C at the bodice side seam, with the corners matching.

6 Then match and pin point B of the sleeve armhole to point B at the bodice side seam, with the corners matching.

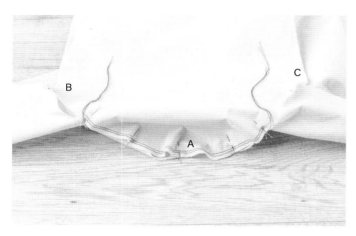

7 Pin from C, towards A until you reach the gathering and stop. Then, pin any notches you may have. Repeat from point B. Make sure always to keep the raw edges together!

8 You should now notice that the remaining sections look slightly bigger on the sleeve than the armhole. You will gently gather the sleeve head to fit the armhole.

At one end of your gathering, wrap the two long end threads around your fingers. Leave the two long threads alone on the other side of the fabric. Holding the fabric, gently pull the threads and you will see the layer of fabric bunch up.

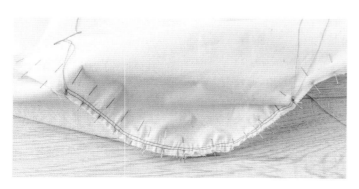

9 Start from one side at a time and gather to the shoulder seam. The beauty of gathering is if you gather too much, you just loosen it to fit. Depending on the style you choose, you might only gather a small amount.

10 Try to spread the gathering equally between sections. It will look wavy on the raw edges but it should sit flat where your stitch line will be. Do not be afraid to overpin.

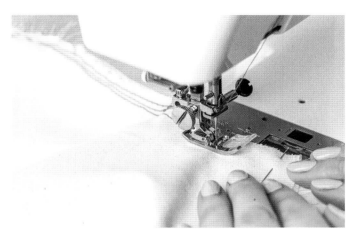

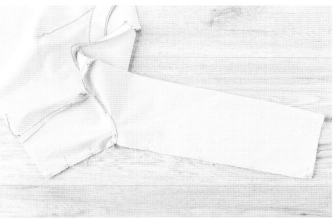

11 When sewing, keep the layers as flat as possible in front of the foot. Check the path is clear before sewing by lifting the foot to see that nothing is catching underneath. Keep checking throughout as sewing curves can be fiddly.

12 Lastly, the sleeve seam and bodice side seams are pinned with the right sides together (**RST**). Make sure you match the underarm seam neatly. Sew the underarm and side seam in one go.

The finished sleeve.

Tips

- *If you have a small tuck in your armhole after sewing, firstly try to ease it out using your nails. If it won't budge, just unpick about 1cm (⅜in) either side of it, wiggle the tuck out and re-sew.*

- *If you add extra fullness into your sleeve, you will focus your gathering at the sleeve head. You will create lots of tucks, which are fine to be sewn, and are a great design feature.*

FLARED SLEEVE

The flared sleeve is a simple shape and design to start with. It is easy to create from your sleeve block and allows you to add minimal flare for a loose fitted sleeve, or maximum flare for a more stylized floaty sleeve.

If using a heavy fabric, a small amount of flare is good, but if you are using a soft floaty fabric, the more flare the better for a soft, romantic look.

Firstly, trace off your sleeve pattern without seam allowance and cut it out. Mark notches and extend the grainline the full length of the sleeve.

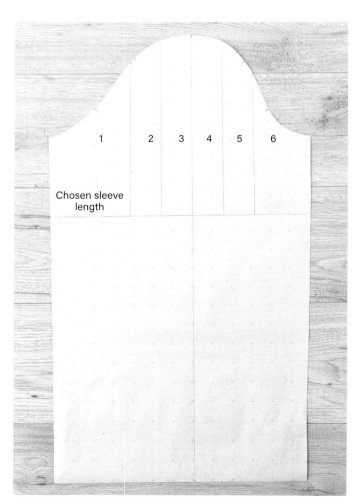

1 Measure how long you want your sleeve to be. Draw a horizontal line across at the chosen length.

Divide your sleeve into six sections by drawing four vertical parallel lines, two on each side of the grainline. Position the lines approximately 4–6cm (1½–2⅜in) apart, depending on the size of the pattern.

2 Cut across the horizontal line.

3 Then cut up each vertical line, including the grainline, but leave the sections attached by a few millimetres at the sleeve head.

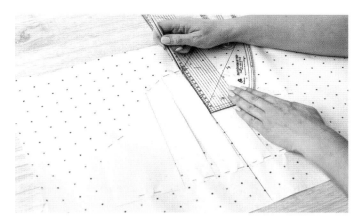

4 Place the sleeve onto a fresh piece of pattern paper. Spread your sleeve out with an equal gap between each section. The gaps can be anything from 1–10cm (⅜–4in), depending on how much flare you want. The example has a gap of 1cm (⅜in) between each section, measured at the lower edge.

Pin each piece in place as you can reuse this pattern piece to change the amount of flare.

Draw a new red grainline in the centre of the middle opening.

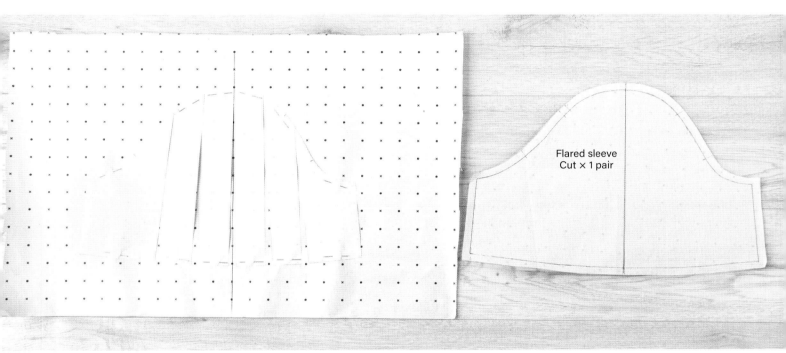

Flared sleeve
Cut × 1 pair

5 Place a new piece of paper over the top and pin in place. Draw around the new pattern, making sure you mark the notches and grainline.

6 Add a 1cm (⅜in) seam allowance the whole way around. Cut out and label your pattern piece with 'Flared Sleeve' and 'cut × 1 pair'.

7 See pages 104–107 for how to sew your sleeve.

Tip

• *Once you create your new sleeve pattern, sew just one sleeve onto the bodice to see how it looks. You can then revisit your pattern if you need to add or reduce fullness.*

CAPPED SLEEVE

The capped sleeve is a small sleeve which extends over the shoulder, giving a little bit of coverage. You can keep it simple and snug to the arm or you can add flare or some extra width to allow a little more room.

In this example, I have chosen to add gathers to the sleeve head to give an extra bit of fullness and shape. If you don't want the gathers, you can just flare it out like the flared sleeve.

Firstly, trace off a short version of your sleeve pattern without seam allowance and cut it out. Mark notches and extend the grainline the full length of the sleeve.

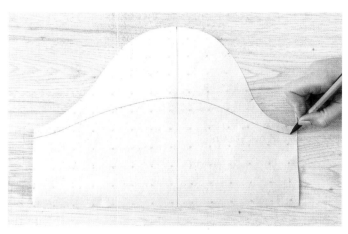

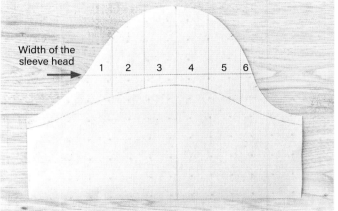

1 Measure how long you want your capped sleeve to be. I measured 10cm (4in) from the sleeve head and kept the underarm 1cm (⅜in) long. You can alter these measurements to suit you.

Draw a gentle curve along the new line of the sleeve.

2 Draw a horizontal line at 90 degrees to the grainline across the width of the sleeve head.

Divide your sleeve into six sections by drawing two vertical parallel lines on each side of the grainline. Position these approximately 4–6cm (1½–2⅜in) apart, depending on the size of the pattern.

Number the sections from 1 to 6.

3 Cut around the outside of the sleeve pattern piece. Cut up each line, including the grainline, to fully separate the pieces.

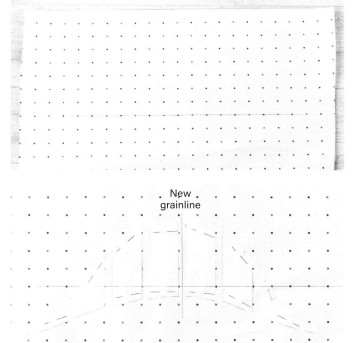

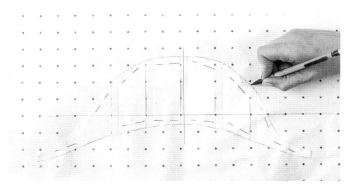

4 Draw a horizontal line onto a fresh piece of pattern paper.

5 Using the horizontal line to keep the pieces level, place the sleeve pieces onto the paper and spread them out with equal gaps. I chose a 1cm (⅜in) gap between each line.

Pin each piece in place, as you can reuse this pattern piece to change the amount of flare.

Draw a new grainline in the centre of the middle opening.

6 Your sleeve head will need to be redrawn with a smooth curve. Place a new piece of paper over the top and pin in place. Draw around the new pattern. Add a 1cm (⅜in) seam allowance all around. Cut out your new pattern piece.

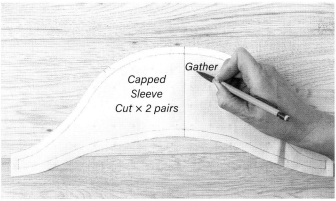

7 Make sure your new underarm seam is at right angles to the straight hem to allow a neat finish when sewing.

8 Your notches will have moved position when you spread out your pattern pieces, so simply mark the Back with two notches approximately 10cm (4in) from the centre notch. Then, mark the Front with one notch approximately 10cm (4in) from the centre notch. Write 'gather' between those notches. Label your pattern piece with 'Capped Sleeve' and 'cut × 2 pairs'.

See the next page for cutting out and sewing your capped sleeve.

Preparing the capped sleeve

As your hem is curved, you will need to cut two sleeve pieces for each side, as it is difficult to neatly turn up a curved edge. Instead, you will be effectively lining your sleeve, starting by sewing the sleeve pieces together at the hem.

If you choose a thick fabric, it will be hard to gather two layers so you will need to straighten out the seam to hem it as normal.

1 Place the 2 × left, or right, sleeve pieces right sides together (**RST**) and pin the hems together, then sew a 1cm (⅜in) seam allowance along the curved hem.

2 Snip into the curved seam allowance, right up to the stitching.

3 Fold the sleeve pieces wrong sides together and press the hem neatly from the right side. You can sew a row of topstitching along the hem if you like. Then pin together the sleeve heads and treat your sleeve as one layer.

If you have one layer of thick fabric, neaten the hem, turn up 1cm (⅜in) towards the inside and press. Then topstitch along the hem to keep it in place. Repeat for the other sleeve.

Fitting the capped sleeve

1 On each sleeve, sew two rows of gathering stitch along the sleeve head, between the front and back notches. Gather the sleevehead so that all of the excess is gathered either side of the centre notch (see pages 104–106).

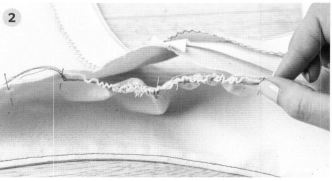

2 Pin your sleeves to your bodice as normal, pinning the side seams and then the centre notch of the sleeve to the shoulder point of the bodice (**RST**). Then pin from the side seams to the notches, keeping the fabric nice and flat. Spread the gathering to fit into the remaining armhole at the sleeve head. The more compact the gathering is at the sleeve head, the more fullness you get at the shoulder. Sew along the sleeve-head seam.

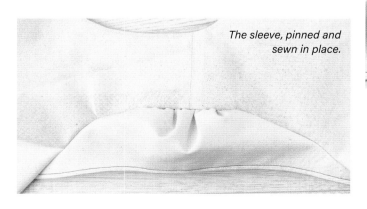

The sleeve, pinned and sewn in place.

PUFF SLEEVE

The puff sleeve gives you fullness at the sleeve head and at the cuff. It can be a short or long sleeve. The puff sleeve can make a simple dress come alive with its dramatic shape. It is also very comfortable to wear with the loose fit on the arm and elastic cuff.

Firstly, trace off your sleeve pattern without seam allowance and cut it out. Mark notches and extend the grainline the full length of the sleeve.

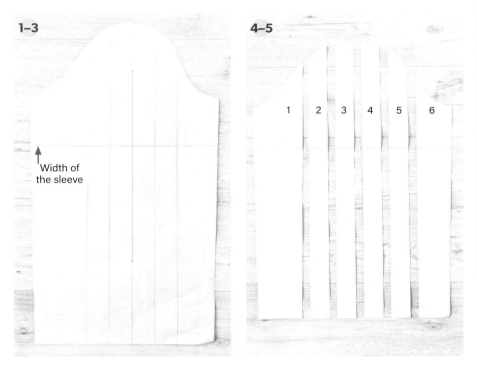

1 Measure how long you want your sleeve to be. Cut to that length.

2 Draw a horizontal line 90 degrees to the grainline across the width of the sleeve.

3 Divide your sleeve into six sections by drawing two vertical parallel lines on each side of the grainline. Position the lines approximately 4–6cm (1½–2⅜in) apart, depending on the size of the pattern.

4 Number the sections from 1 to 6.

5 Cut all the way up each line, including the grainline, to open out each section.

6 Draw a horizontal line onto a fresh piece of pattern paper. Place the sleeve pieces onto the paper, lining up the horizontal lines. Spread your pieces out with equal gaps of anything from 1–10cm (⅜–4in), depending on how much flare you want. You can have less flare at the sleeve head.

Pin each piece in place as you can reuse this pattern piece to change the amount of flare.

7 Draw a new grainline in the centre of the middle opening. Place a new piece of paper over the top and pin in place. Draw around the new pattern. Your sleeve head will need to be redrawn with a smooth curve.

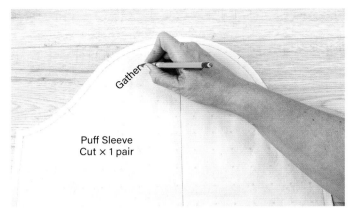

Puff Sleeve
Cut × 1 pair

8 Your notches will have moved position when you spread out your pattern pieces, so simply mark the Back with two notches approximately 10cm (4in) from the centre notch. Then, mark the Front with one notch approximately 10cm (4in) from the centre notch. Write 'gather' between those notches.

Add 1cm (⅜in) seam allowance on the sleeve head and side seams but 2cm (¾in) on the hem. Cut out and label your pattern piece with 'Puff Sleeve' and 'cut × 1 pair'.

9 On each side of the hem, mark a notch 1cm (⅜in) up from the bottom edge and also 2cm (¾in) up from the edge. In between these notches write 'leave gap'.

Sewing the puff sleeve

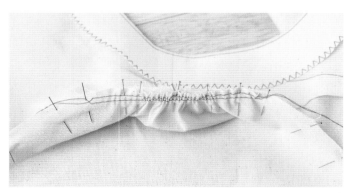

1 On each sleeve, sew two rows of gathering stitch along the sleeve head between the notches (see pages 104–105). Pin your sleeves to your bodice as normal, pinning the side seams and then pinning the centre notch of the sleeve to the shoulder point of the bodice (**RST**). Pin from the side seams to the notches, nice and flat. Then gather the sleeve head to fit either side of the centre notch. This gives a lovely fullness at the shoulder. Sew the sleeve into place.

2 Neaten the hem of the sleeve.

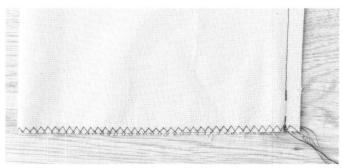

3 Sew the side seams of the sleeve and bodice, making sure to leave the gap at the sleeve hem.

The gap in the side seam will allow you to thread a length of thin elastic into a channel once hemmed.

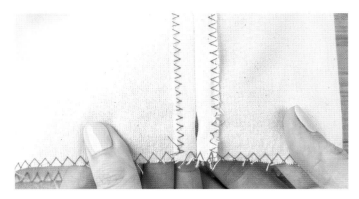

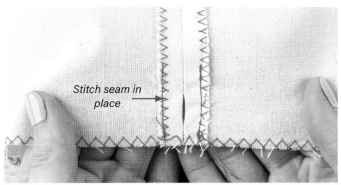

Stitch seam in place

4 Press the sleeve seams open and neaten the seam allowances separately.

5 Stitch each seam allowance in place with a few stitches along the edge. This will help when you are threading the elastic at step 7.

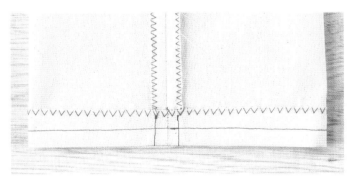

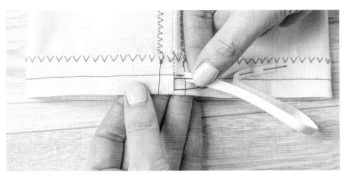

6 Fold up the 2cm (¾in) hem and pin in place. Sew a row of stitching around each cuff, 1cm (⅜in) from the hem. This creates the channel for your elastic.

7 Attach a safety pin on one end of the elastic. Pin the other end to the sleeve, so it doesn't get pulled into the channel. Thread the elastic through the channel in the hem. My elastic was 22cm (8⅝in) long.

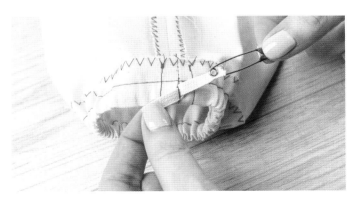

8 Once you pull the safety pin out of the channel, overlap the ends of the elastic by 1cm (⅜in) and sew together.

9 Lastly, stretch the cuff and the elastic will pop through the gap into the channel. Close the stitching gap with a few hand-stitches.

BUTTERFLY SLEEVE

The butterfly sleeve is a beautiful, decorative sleeve, with frills that resemble a butterfly's wings. The sleeve can be mid length and floaty or short and defined. The fullness added and fabrics used will change the look of the sleeve quite dramatically. You can use the traditional method of slash and spread (see page 108) or you can use a mathematical method. It depends on how you prefer to work. The rounder the circle, the more fullness you will have.

Traditional method

Firstly, trace off a short version of your sleeve pattern without seam allowance and cut it out. Mark notches and extend the grainline the full length of the sleeve.

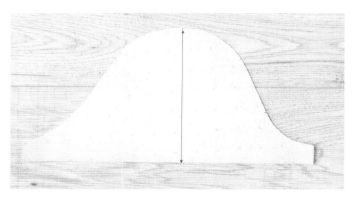

1 Cut the sleeve pattern to your required length. I measured 8cm (3⅛in) from the sleeve head, with the underarm 1.5cm (⅝in) long. You can alter these measurements to suit you.

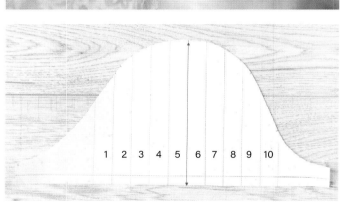

2 Draw a horizontal line across your armhole from side seam to side seam. Divide your sleeve into at least 10 sections by drawing parallel vertical lines each side of the grainline. Position these approximately 2–4cm (¾–1½in) apart, depending on the size of the pattern. Number the sections from 1 to 10 and cut up the vertical lines, leaving them attached by a couple of millimetres at the top.

3 Place the sleeve onto a fresh piece of pattern paper. Fan your sleeve out generously, creating a circle in the centre (see opposite, top left and top right). Make sure there is enough room to add a seam allowance on both side seams. Pin each piece in place, as you can reuse this pattern piece to change the amount of flare.

Trace off the new pattern piece and add 1cm (⅜in) seam allowances all the way around.

Cut out and label your pattern piece with 'Butterfly Sleeve' and 'cut × 1 pair.'

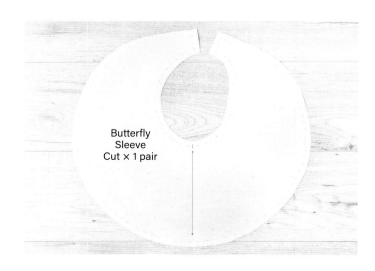

Butterfly
Sleeve
Cut × 1 pair

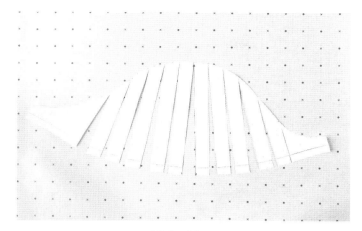

Minimal flare

If you slash and spread the pieces out with minimal spacing, you will get a gentle flare in your sleeve.

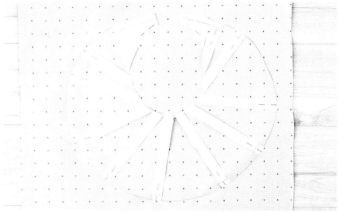

Maximum Flare

By slashing and spreading the pieces fully, the armhole becomes circular and your sleeve will be full of flare.

Mathematical method

This method allows you to draw a perfect circle, with the circumference of the circle being the same measurement as the length of the armhole.

To draw a perfect circle, you need to know the circumference and the radius.

The armhole measurement plus seam allowance = the circumference

Radius = Circumference divided by 6.28 (π × 2)

Example

Armhole measurement = 47.5cm (18¾in)

Seam allowance = 2cm (¾in) for both side seams

Circumference = 47.5cm (18¾in) + 2cm (¾in) = 49.5cm (19½in)

Radius: 49.5cm (19½in) divided by 6.28 = 7.88cm (3⅛in)

1 Using both the Front and Back Bodice blocks without seam allowances, measure the exact armhole. Place the tape measure on its side so it allows you to measure curves accurately to the millimetre.

2 Add 2cm (¾in) to your armhole measurement to find your circumference.

Continued overleaf.

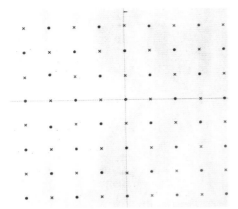

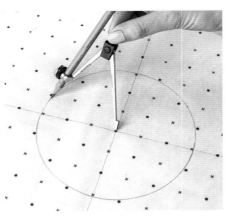

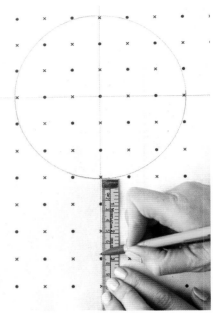

3 Draw a line down the centre of your pattern paper. Square across at the middle.

4 Using a pair of compasses set at the radius measurement, place the point in the middle of the cross. Draw a full circle. This should equal your circumference.

5 Measure the length of the sleeve and mark on the vertical line below the circle.

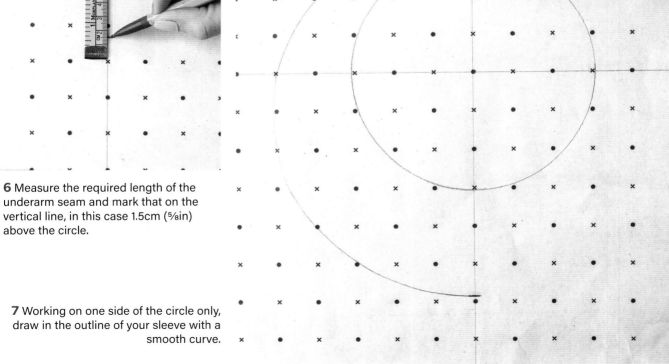

6 Measure the required length of the underarm seam and mark that on the vertical line, in this case 1.5cm (⅝in) above the circle.

7 Working on one side of the circle only, draw in the outline of your sleeve with a smooth curve.

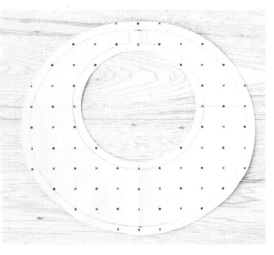

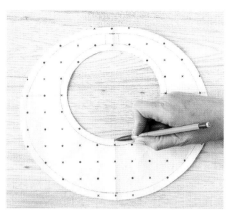

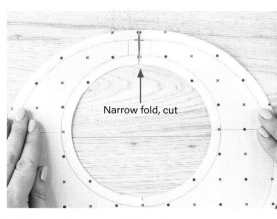

Narrow fold, cut

8 Add the seam allowance to the outside curve and then also the inside curve.

9 Fold the paper in half along the vertical line and pin securely in place. Cut around your new design, which will be symmetrical when opened out.

10 Mark the centre on the inside curve. This will be matched up to the shoulder seam on the bodice. The pattern piece is symmetrical so there is no 'front' or 'back'.

11 Cut on the narrow fold at the top to separate the pattern piece at the underarm.

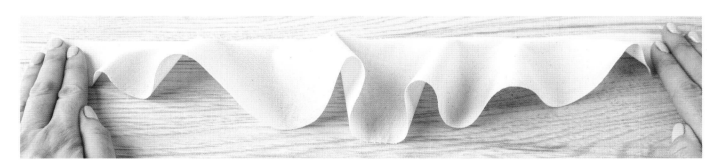

12 When you cut your sleeve out in fabric, the circular armhole creates a fabulous frill in the fabric when opened out straight. The sleeve is inserted as shown on pages 104–106, without the gathering.

13 If your sleeve is too full, you can take some fullness out by making small folds in the pattern, at the outer edge of the circle. Make sure you don't take anything off the inner circle.

How to make this outfit
This beautiful, printed cotton skirt is gathered at the waist with a narrow waistband (see pages 126 and 156). It is paired with a soft cotton top (page 154) with a curved neckline (page 94) and butterfly sleeves (page 116). There is a second layer of butterfly sleeves to add extra frill. The top made in satin could be paired with a crepe skirt, transforming this into an evening-wear look.

How to make this dress

This dress is my favourite shape, with the sweetheart neckline (see page 96), butterfly sleeves (page 116) and full circle skirt (page 128). You can wear an underskirt underneath to add extra volume. It could be made in satin for a perfect evening-wear dress, or black wool for a stunning Little Black Dress.

skirts

The skirt shape changes the whole vibe of a dress. You can have so much fun with volume and length to create some beautiful silhouettes. You can keep the dress as a classic straight dress or you can go wild and add a full circle skirt.

For each of the five skirt shape options – **fitted, gathered, circle, A-line and pleated** – I will guide you through how to draft the pattern.

In the first instance I will show you how to make up each type of skirt; on pages 156–158, I explain how to add a waistband or facing.

To incorporate the skirt into a dress, the skirt will be sewn onto the waistline of the bodice, which is explained opposite.

Finally, you will learn how to finish your garment with a zip, on page 146.

The beauty of this book is that once you create the skirt patterns, you can either add a simple waistband to create a range of skirts and/or turn them into dresses. Watch your wardrobe grow while you play with the shapes!

Fitted skirt
See below

Gathered skirt
See page 126

Circle skirt
See page 128

A-line skirt
See page 130

Box-pleated skirt
See page 132

FITTED SKIRT

We start simple by creating a fitted skirt. Using a heavier fabric such as denim, will create a bold silhouette; you can play with the length and fit but don't make it too tight around your knees, to allow for ease of movement.

When adding the fitted skirt to the bodice, the waistline will be accentuated. You can be brave and use different fabrics for the top and lower sections for a statement look, or stick to a single fabric for a streamlined appearance.

You have two options when drafting a fitted skirt:

Option 1 You can alter the skirt block to make a fitted skirt; this can be attached to the bodice.

Option 2 You can remove the waistline seam by joining the bodice patterns to the skirt patterns at the waistline, creating one long pattern piece for both the front and the back.

Both options are explained on pages 123–125. Note that the fitted skirt is the only style that you can merge with the bodice blocks to make a full dress pattern, as the darts must remain in the skirt.

Option 1 – Creating a skirt, which can be attached to the bodice

1 Draw a horizontal line across your paper. Place your skirt front and skirt back patterns alongside each other with the hip line exactly on the horizontal line. Leave approximately 10–12.5cm (4–5in) between the patterns at the side seam.

2 Trace both pattern pieces without seam allowance, making sure you mark all notches and darts etc.

3 Decide on the length of your skirt. The Skirt Block is knee-length on a woman of average height in the UK – 161.5cm (5ft 3in). Measure from your waist to the desired length, then you can shorten or lengthen as you need. Just make sure that whatever measurement you add or subtract, it is exactly the same the whole way around the hem. Also, remember to allow extra for your hem allowances.

Option 2 – Merging the bodice and skirt patterns to make a complete dress without a waistline

1 Draw a horizontal line across your paper. Place your Front and Back Bodice pieces alongside each other with the bust line exactly on the horizontal line. Leave approximately 10–12.5cm (4–5in) between the patterns at the side seam.

2 Trace off both pattern pieces without seam allowance, making sure you mark all notches and darts, and so on.

3 Continue the centre-front line vertically, down the paper.

4 Position the Front Skirt so the centre-front seam sits on the vertical line and the waistlines meet. The darts should match up and the side seams too. Position the Back Skirt in the same way.

5 Trace the Front and Back Skirt, marking all of the notches, darts and so on.

6 Decide on the length of your dress. Shorten or lengthen as you need.

Continued for both options overleaf.

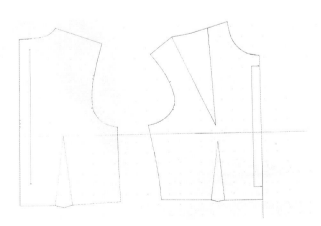

Continue for both options

- Find the widest part on the skirt and draw a horizontal line across both patterns. Usually this is the hip line or lower, so you can start to take in the skirt patterns from here.

- Choose how much you want to take off from around the hem and mark each side seam equally. Start with approximately 1cm (⅜in) off each side seam as this will take 4cm (1½in) in total. See page 56.

- Draw a straight line from the widest part down to the mark at the hem. Then smooth the line at the hip to reflect the gentle curve of your hips.

- You can also take in the centre-back seam by 1.5cm (⅝in), which will allow you to create a well-fitted skirt. Just make sure that you can sit down in the skirt if you go for a tighter fit.

- Your zip needs to open to the widest part of the skirt section, being your hips and bottom. This allows you to get the skirt on and off easily. Mark this point with a notch and write on the pattern 'zip opening to here'.

- Add seam allowances to the new patterns except for the centre front as this will be placed on the fold. Cut out your new pattern pieces.

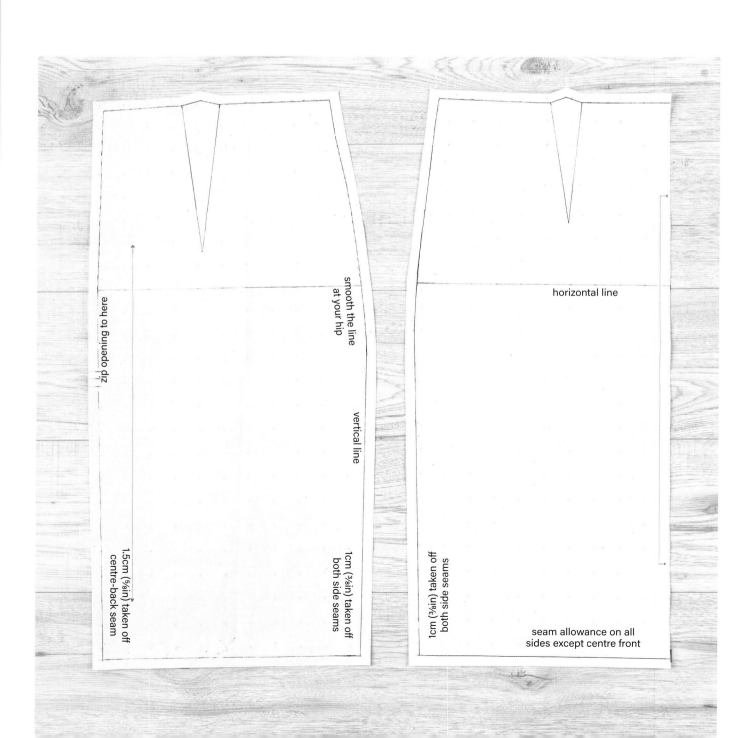

zip opening to here

smooth the line at your hip

horizontal line

vertical line

1.5cm (⅝in) taken off centre-back seam

1cm (⅜in) taken off both side seams

1cm (⅜in) taken off both side seams

seam allowance on all sides except centre front

HOW TO SEW THE FITTED SKIRT

1 Prepare and sew the darts.

2 Pin and sew the side seams together. Neaten the seam allowances together.

3 Pin and sew up the centre-back seam to the zip opening. Neaten the seam allowances open.

4 Attach a facing or waistband (I prefer a facing on a fitted skirt) – see pages 156–158.

5 Insert the zip (see page 146).

6 Hem the skirt (see page 144).

To sew the skirt onto the bodice to make a dress, follow steps 1 and 2, then go to page 144.

HOW TO SEW THE FITTED DRESS

1 Prepare and sew the darts.

2 Pin and sew the shoulder seams. Neaten the seam allowances together.

3 Attach the facings to the neckline.

4 Attach the facings to the armhole or attach the sleeves.

5 Pin and sew the side seams together. Neaten the seam allowances together.

6 Pin and sew up the centre-back seam to the zip opening. Neaten the seam allowances open.

7 Insert the zip (see page 146).

8 Hem the dress (see page 144).

GATHERED SKIRT

You can have lots of fun with a gathered skirt as it is totally up to you how much fullness you want to create.

I recommend using a lightweight fabric as you will get a gorgeous, full gathered effect. You can play with the length and create a shorter skirt which will appear fuller, or make it longer and let the fabric drape from the gathers.

I would avoid using a heavy fabric such as denim as you will struggle to gather it and it will add bulk to the waistline.

Be mindful of your fabric choice as some fabric prints have a direction to them, so all of your pattern pieces need to be placed on the fabric the correct way up. Make sure the print doesn't appear upside down on any pieces.

Measure the hip line on either the Front or Back Skirt pattern piece, as the measurements will be similar.

- For a good amount of gathering, double the hip-line measurement.
- For very full gathering, triple the hip-line measurement.

Drawing your pattern piece

When you have your hip-line measurement, draw a rectangle the width of which is that same amount. The height will equal the length of the skirt – this measurement is for you to decide, but bear in mind that you will also need to add a hem allowance to the total length.

- Add a seam allowance to the top, bottom and one side. The other side will be the centre front. **You will use this pattern piece for both the front and the back.** You can add an extra 1cm (⅜in) seam allowance when cutting the backs but it isn't vital.

- When cutting out the front, place one side on the fold of the fabric and cut around the rest. Mark the centre front with a notch.

- When cutting out the backs, cut two pieces out fully.

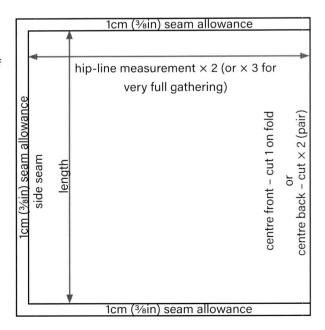

In the diagram:

1cm (⅜in) seam allowance

hip-line measurement × 2 (or × 3 for very full gathering)

1cm (⅜in) seam allowance

side seam

length

centre front – cut 1 on fold
or
centre back – cut × 2 (pair)

1cm (⅜in) seam allowance

HOW TO SEW THE GATHERED SKIRT

1 Pin and sew the side seams (**RST**). Press open.

2 Neaten your side seam allowances together and the centre-back seam allowances separately.

Gathering the sections

• Set your sewing machine to the longest stitch length. Do not backstitch for gathering!

• Leaving your starting and end threads long, sew two parallel rows of stitching along the top of each panel. Start and stop near to the seam itself but don't catch the seam allowance.

• The first row of stitching should be 5mm (¼in) from the edge of the fabric.

• For the second row of stitching, for a 1cm (⅜in) seam allowance, sew 1.25cm (½in) from the edge; for a 1.5cm (⅝in) seam allowance, sew 1cm (⅜in) from the edge. Don't stitch over your gathering rows as the gathering thread becomes harder to remove.

• To gather, work on one panel at a time. Tie your threads together at one end to allow the gathering to go right up to the knot. Hold the opposite two upper (or lower) thread ends together and gently slide the fabric along the threads, towards the knots.

• You can knot the other ends when you have gathered the correct amount. This allows you to spread the gathers evenly between the knots.

Attaching the skirt to a bodice or waistband

If attaching to a bodice, the neck facing and sleeves must be attached first. See pages 142–144.

1 Placing the right sides together (**RST**), pin the skirt to the bodice or waistband at the side seams, centre-back seams and centre front.

2 Spread the gathering equally to fit each section. Make sure the raw edges are neatly together.

3 Pin in place and sew a 1cm (⅜in) seam allowance. Pull out the gathering threads if they are visible on the front.

4 Pin and sew up the centre-back seam to the zip opening. Neaten the seam allowances open.

5 Insert the zip (see page 146).

6 Hem the skirt (see page 144).

CIRCLE SKIRT

There are a few methods to create a circle skirt, depending on the fullness you require. As with the butterfly sleeve on page 116, you can use the traditional method of slash and spread (see page 108) or, again, a mathematical method. The rounder the circle, the more fullness you will have. To keep things simple, I will show you the mathematic method, which will add maximum fullness to your Front and Back Skirt pattern pieces.

You will create a separate pattern piece for both the Front and the Back Skirt. The method is the same for both. The front and back finished pattern pieces will each be a quarter of the skirt to save creating large pattern pieces, which can be difficult to manage.

You will place your front pattern piece on the fold as normal, and cut two of your back pattern pieces as normal.

Your finished skirt will have side seams and a centre-back seam, so the construction method is the same as for every skirt in this book.

Don't let the mathematics put you off as, once you create the pattern, it is super-easy to sew together. You only need the waist measurement of the pattern piece and your chosen length of the skirt. Then, just follow the instructions and you will have a full circle skirt in no time.

Measuring the waistline

Start with the Front Skirt pattern piece, then repeat the steps using the Back Skirt pattern piece.

- First, close the dart on the pattern piece.

- Measure the waistline without seam allowance. Place the tape measure on its side so it allows you to measure curves to the millimetre accurately.

- Make a note of the measurement on the pattern piece.

Mathematical method

To draw a quarter of a circle, you first need to work out the radius, based on your waistline measurement.

In the example on the left, the waistline measurement of the pattern piece is 20.5cm (8in) – this is one-quarter of the full waistline.

Radius = Waistline measurement × 2 ÷ 3.14 (this is π)

So, for this example, the radius = (20.5cm [8in] × 2 = 41cm [16⅛in]) ÷ 3.14 (π) = **13.06cm [5⅛in]**

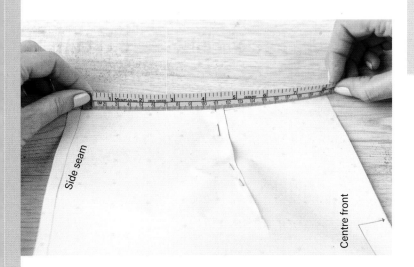

DRAWING THE CIRCLE SKIRT

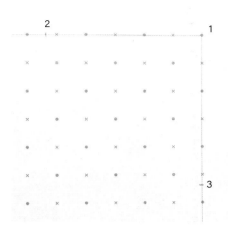

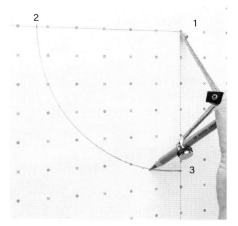

Tip
• *If you want to decrease the fullness, you can refer to step 13 on page 119.*

1 Mark number 1 on your paper, which is at the centre of an imaginary circle. Square down and then across. The lines should measure as follows:
  ◆ 1 to 2 = The radius
  ◆ 1 to 3 = The radius

2 If you have a pair of compasses, set them at the radius measurement. Place the point in the corner at 1 and draw a quarter-circle from 2 to 3. The length of this curve from 2–3 should equal the waistline measurement (in this example, 20.5cm/8in).
  If you don't have compasses, use something round to help you draw the curved line from 2–3.

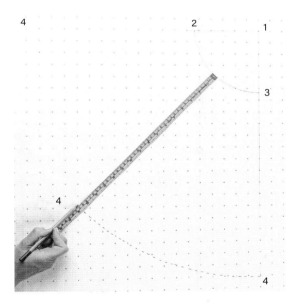

3 Using a metre ruler or tape measure, mark in the skirt length twice between the following points:
  ◆ 2 to 4 = Skirt length (including hem allowance)
  ◆ 3 to 4 = Skirt length (including hem allowance)

4 For the Front, add in a seam allowance on one of the sides and mark the other side as 'cut on the fold.' Then add the seam allowance on the waistline curve.

5 For the Back, add in seam allowances on both sides. Then add the seam allowance on the waistline curve.

HOW TO SEW THE CIRCLE SKIRT

1 Cut one front piece on the fold and two back pieces. Pin and sew the side seams together. Neaten the seam allowances together.

2 Pin and sew up the centre back seam to the zip opening. Neaten the seam allowances open.

3 Attach a waistband if making a separate skirt (see pages 156–159).

4 Insert the zip (see page 146).

5 Hem the skirt. Be aware that some fabrics might not hang evenly, even though the length is perfect on the paper. Let the fabric hang over a few days and the hem will drop into place. You can re-hem it if needed.

For instructions on how to sew a skirt onto a bodice to make a dress, go to page 144.

A-LINE SKIRT

The A-line skirt is a classic shape which is comfortable to wear. You can easily remove the darts for a simplistic shape which is really quick to make.

You don't need much fabric and can have fun with the fabric you use. A soft fabric will hang gently and a firmer fabric will hold the A-line shape.

The fullness is added into the side seams and also the centre-back seam to create the flared shape.

1–3

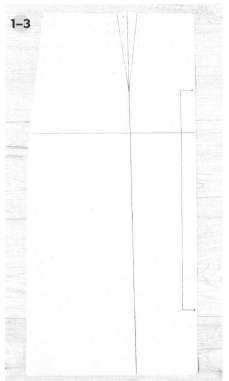

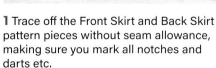

4–5

Front Skirt

Hip line

Grainline

1 Trace off the Front Skirt and Back Skirt pattern pieces without seam allowance, making sure you mark all notches and darts etc.

2 Cut out both pattern pieces. Start with the Front Skirt.

3 Draw a vertical line through the centre of the dart and continue the line straight down to the hem.

4 Cut up the vertical line from the hem, stopping at the base of the dart.

5 Close the dart and pin in place. This will flare out the lower part of the skirt.

6 Retrace the skirt pattern onto a fresh piece of paper with plenty of room around it. Mark in the hip line and the grainline and add the name of the pattern piece and the size.

Hip line

7 Using a long ruler, starting at the hip line or slightly higher, flare out the side seam. You want this line to be straight.

8 Soften the hemline to a gentle curve.

9 Add seam allowances and cut out the pattern piece.

Repeat for the Back Skirt.

HOW TO SEW THE A-LINE SKIRT

1 Cut one front piece on the fold, and two back pieces. Pin and sew the side seams together. Neaten the seam allowances together.

2 Pin and sew up the centre-back seam to the zip opening. Neaten the seam allowances open.

3 Attach a facing or a waistband (see pages 156–158) if you are making a separate skirt.

4 Insert the zip (see page 146).

5 Hem the skirt (see page 144).

For instructions on how to sew a skirt onto a bodice to make a dress, go to page 144.

BOX-PLEATED SKIRT

Once you have removed your darts and flared your skirt patterns to create an A-line skirt (see pages 130–131) you can then add in some fun pleats, which really add character to your skirt. This is a lot easier to do than you might think so give it a go!

When you come to choose your final fabric, use a cotton or firmer fabric, which will hold the shape beautifully. Be careful when choosing any prints as you need to be really accurate with stripes. Remember you will lose some fabric inside the pleat so think about your pattern placement.

I have used 3cm (1⅛in) for the width of each pleat. You can decrease or increase the pleat however much you like. Practise folding the pleat on the paper pattern to see how it works and to gauge the size.

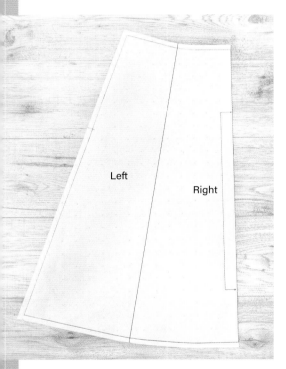
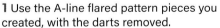

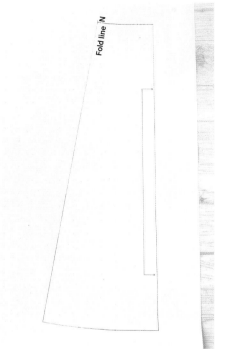

1 Use the A-line flared pattern pieces you created, with the darts removed.

2 On both the front and the back pattern pieces, mark the centre of the waistline and then the centre of the hem. Draw a vertical line down the centre of the patterns.

3 Mark Left and Right on the pattern pieces either side of the vertical line.

4 Starting with the Front Skirt piece, trace off the Right side of the pattern piece, not including the seam allowance. Leave plenty of room around the pattern piece.

5 At the top of the vertical line, label as 'Fold Line' and mark a notch.

6 Draw a line 3cm (1⅛in) parallel to the left of the vertical line. Label as 'Fold Line' and mark a notch (shown by N in the diagram above).

7 Draw a line 3cm (1⅛in) parallel to the left of the new line. Label as 'Centre' and mark a notch.

8 Draw a line 3cm (1⅛in) parallel to the left of the new line. Label as 'Fold Line' and mark a notch.

9 Draw a line 3cm (1⅛in) parallel to the left of the new line. Label as 'Fold line' and mark a notch.

10 Square across from the waistline and then the hemline.

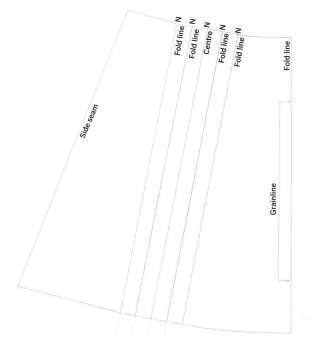

11 Now line up the Left side of the skirt on the last drawn vertical line. Make sure you line up the waistline and hemline. Trace around the Left side.

At this stage, if you would like to add a pleat in the centre front, you will need to add half the pleat onto the centre-front edge as your pattern is cut on the fold.

a On the centre fold, label as 'fold line' and mark a notch.

b Square across from the waistline and then the hemline.

c Draw a line 3cm (1¼in) parallel to the right of the centre-front edge. Label as 'fold line' and mark a notch.

d Draw a line 3cm (1¼in) parallel to the right of the new line. Label as 'centre' and mark a notch. Also write 'cut on fold.'

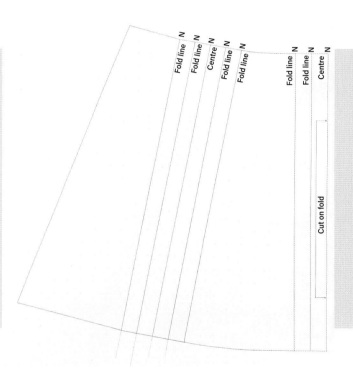

12 Label the side seam and centre front on the pattern.

13 Add seam allowances and cut out the pattern.
Repeat this with the Back Skirt piece but don't add a pleat onto the centre back seam as it will make your zip fastening much harder to sew into the seam).

HOW TO SEW THE A-LINE SKIRT WITH BOX PLEATS

1 Cut one Front piece on the fold and two Back pieces. Prepare and secure the pleats in place with a row of tacking (basting) stitches within the seam allowance. Make sure your raw edges all sit in line on your waistline for a neat finish. (See below.)

2 Pin and sew the side seams together. Neaten the seam allowances together.

3 Pin and sew up the centre-back seam to the zip opening. Neaten the seam allowances open.

4 Attach a waistband (see pages 156–158).

5 Insert the zip (see page 146).

6 Hem the skirt (see page 144).

For how to sew a skirt onto a bodice to make a dress, go to page 144.

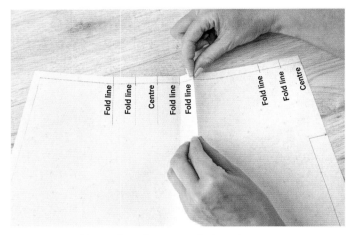

Fold your first pleat as marked on the pattern.

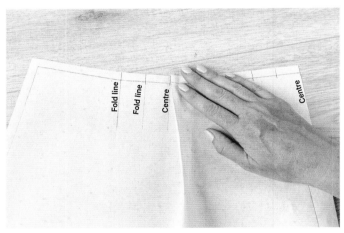

Fold on the right fold line, and fold it over so the fold sits exactly on the centre line. Pin in place.

Repeat on the left side to create your box pleat.

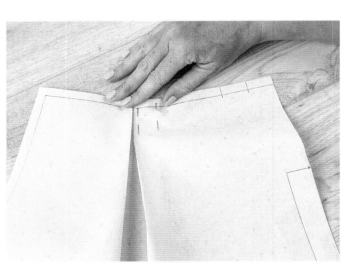

Keep the raw edges in line with each other.

How to make this outfit
This is a simple A-line skirt with the darts removed, which creates a flattering fit (see page 130). It has a facing attached (see page 158). The floral cotton is paired with a plain cotton top (page 154) with a curved neckline (page 94) and soft butterfly sleeves (page 116). A heavy denim could be used for the skirt to totally change the look, along with a printed cotton top.

collars

A collar is a simple but very attractive addition to a garment. You can have fun with fabrics or keep it stylish and matching. Drafting and making a collar is relatively easy, so why not give it a go?

I have chosen to demonstrate a simple Peter Pan collar here.

1 You need your Front and Back Bodice patterns without seam allowances.

2 Draft a curved neckline (see page 94). Keep your neckline quite high when adding a collar.

3 Close the dart on the Front Bodice.

4 Match the neck points exactly but overlap the shoulder points by approximately 2cm (¾in), to allow the collar to hug your shoulder.

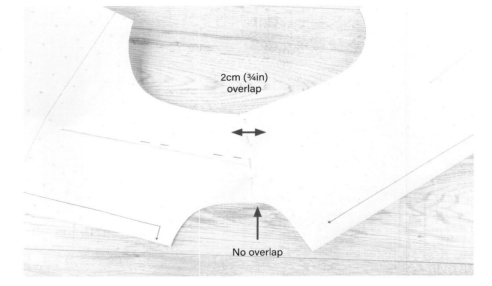

2cm (¾in) overlap

No overlap

5 Draw your collar onto the neckline. Place the paper pattern on yourself, and look in a mirror, to help get the proportions of the collar right for you.

6 Trace off your collar. Mark in your shoulder point on the neckline and label your pattern piece with 'cut × 4.'

7 Add a seam allowance all the way around.

8 Place the pattern piece on yourself or on your dress on a mannequin to see how it looks.

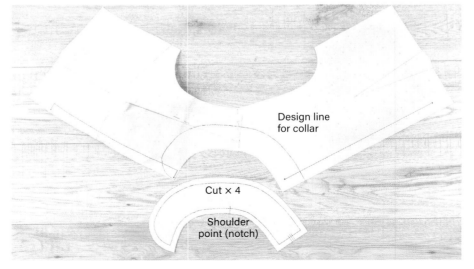

Design line for collar

Cut × 4

Shoulder point (notch)

CUTTING OUT AND SEWING YOUR COLLAR

1 Block fuse your fabric with mediumweight interfacing (see Facings, page 100). If your fabric is thick, fuse just the top layer.

2 Cut out the four collar pieces as two mirrored pairs.

3 Place each collar with the right sides together (**RST**) and pin around the outer edge seams.

4 Sew from the front around to the centre-back seam, and up to the neckline.

5 Snip into the curved edge of your seam allowance to allow the collar to sit flat when turned the right way out. Make sure you cut right up to the seam allowance. Cut a 'V' at tight curves.

6 Trim the centre-back corner seam allowance.

7 Turn the collars the right way out and run your finger along the seam to push the curve out. Poke the corners out to a point.

8 When pressing your collar, iron from the underside. Try to pull the seam allowance fully out, then, roll the under layer away from the seam edge by a few millimetres. Press as you go with steam.

9 You will now see that the seam edges don't align on the inner curve, which is good, as it means you shouldn't see your under-collar from the top. On the inner curve, trim off the excess fabric so it is flush with the edges, then pin the two layers together.

ATTACHING YOUR COLLAR TO YOUR DRESS

1 Pin the collar onto your dress neckline, starting at the centre front, right sides facing up.

2 Pin the shoulder point.

3 Then pin the back, 1cm (⅜in) or 1.5cm (⅝in) in from the centre back, depending on your chosen seam allowance.

4 Pin in between. If your neckline has stretched, just ease it back in to fit the collar.

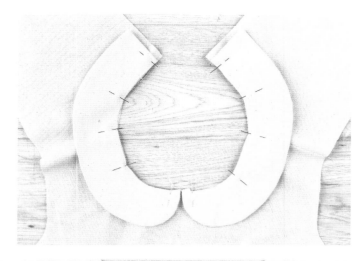

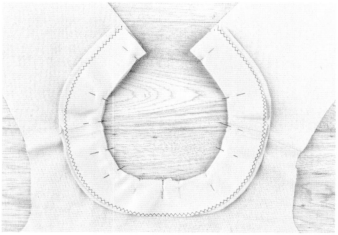

The neckline with the seam stitched.

5 Make a facing for your neckline (see pages 98–100). Place your facing on to your neckline, with the right sides together (**RST**), sandwiching the collar in the middle. Continue to sew your facing as normal (see pages 98–101). Snip into the seam and then understitch (see page 102).

6 Press from the inside of the neckline.

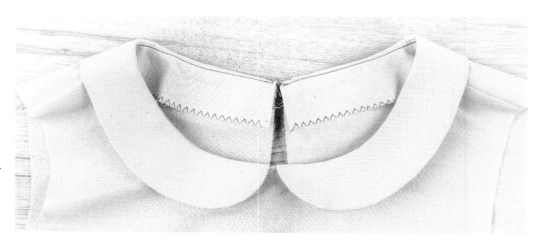

The finished, pressed collar in place.

Pockets

When someone compliments me on a dress, one of my favourite responses is, 'it has pockets!' Pockets are wonderful as for some of us they are simply practical but for others, it's somewhere to prop your hand, which just feels right – if you know what I mean!

Pattern cutting a simple pocket is relatively easy and quick to do. You just add it into your side seams and you are ready to go.

DRAFTING A SIDE-SEAM POCKET

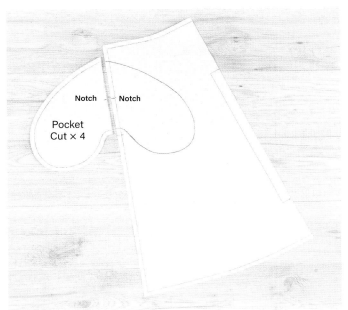

1 Use your Front Skirt pattern with seam allowance. If you are right handed, use your left hand to draw around, and vice versa.

2 Place your hand flat on the skirt pattern at a 45-degree angle to the side seam, as this is how your hand will sit in the pocket. Place the pattern on yourself to help with positioning.

3 Starting approximately 2–3cm (¾–1¼in) down from the waistline, draw around your hand with about 2.5cm (1in) spare all the way around.

4 Curve the line back to the side seam so it is at a right angle to the seam.

5 Draw a notch on the side seam halfway up the pocket.

6 Transfer the notch onto the Front and Back Skirt pattern pieces also, by laying the side seams together.

7 Trace off your pocket piece and add a 1cm (⅜in) seam allowance around the pocket, but not on the side seam as it has it already.

8 Cut out your pattern piece and label it with the name and 'cut × 4'.

SEWING THE POCKET

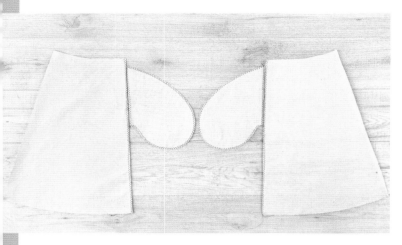

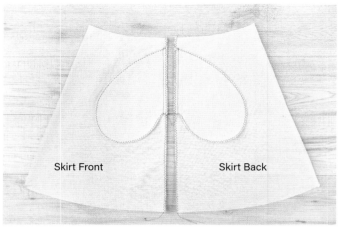

Skirt Front   Skirt Back

1 Neaten the seam allowances of each skirt side seam **separately**.

2 Neaten around the whole of each pocket.

3 With the right sides together (**RST**), place one of each pocket piece on each side seam of the Front and Back Skirt pieces. Match the notches on the side seams.

4 Sew along the length of the pocket on each side seam, taking a fractionally narrower seam allowance (1–2mm) than you are using on the side seams of the skirt pieces.

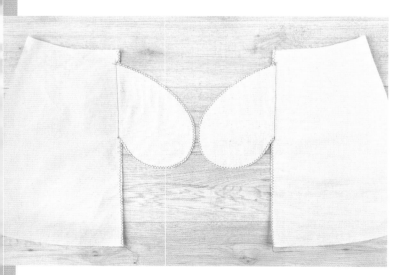

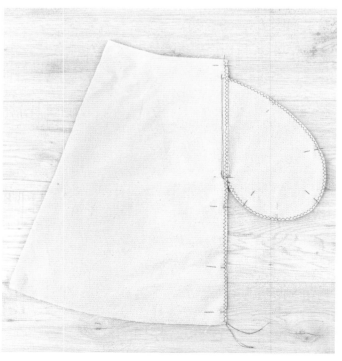

5 Press the pocket away from the skirt so the seamline sits flat. Repeat for each pocket.

6 On each pocket, stitch the length of the pocket, close to the seamline, through the pocket and seam allowances to secure in place. Use understitching (see page 102). This helps to prevent the pocket pieces from showing in the finished garment.

7 Match the Front Skirt to the Back Skirt at the side seams and pin in place.

8 Sew the side seams as normal until you reach the pocket. Sew approximately 1cm (⅜in) past the raw edge of the pocket, then pivot and turn to follow around the pocket edge. (The stitching is shown here in blue, for clarity.)

9 Continue sewing around the pocket curve, pivoting as you go.

10 When you meet the side seam again, pivot and continue along the skirt side seam down to the hem.

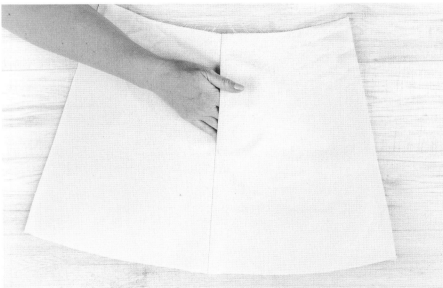

11 Place the skirt so the right sides are facing you. Press your side seams so they sit flat. Make sure your pocket sits to the front of the skirt.

Note

You can't put a pocket in a side seam that will have a zip; your skirt needs to have a centre-back opening.

7 finishing your dress

When you have perfected your fit and chosen the style of your dress, you will sew up your garment in a slightly different order from your sample (toile).

constructing your garment

On your finished garment, it is important to press your seams and then neaten them as you go. As with your sample (toile), you can make your dress with the zip in the centre back, or in the side seam. The order for sewing the zip into the side seam follows on page 144.

SEWING YOUR BODICE TOGETHER

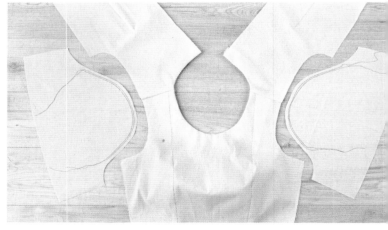

1 Sew all of your darts first. Press your front darts towards the side seams and your back darts towards the centre seam. Pin them in place along your seam edges.

2 Pin and sew the shoulder seams (**RST**). Neaten together.

3 Pin and sew the shoulder seams of your facings. Then pin and sew your facings onto the neckline. Neaten the facing edge and then understitch (see pages 98–102).

4 Sew rows of gathering on your sleeve heads.

How to make this dress ⊢────────

This printed, floral cotton dress consists of an A-line skirt with beautiful box pleats (see page 132), a 'V'-shaped neckline (page 95) and simple flared sleeves (page 108). The shape is simple yet so flattering. You could make it in a denim for a classic daywear dress or use denim for the skirt and a floral cotton for the top to mix up the look.

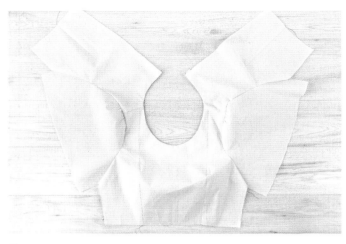

5 Pin and sew your chosen sleeve, or facing, onto the armhole (**RST**). Neaten.

6 Pin and sew up your side and sleeve seams (**RST**). Neaten.

SEWING YOUR SKIRT SECTION TOGETHER

1 Pin and sew the Front Skirt to the Back Skirt at the side seams (**RST**). Neaten the seam allowances together. Neaten the centre-back seam allowances separately.

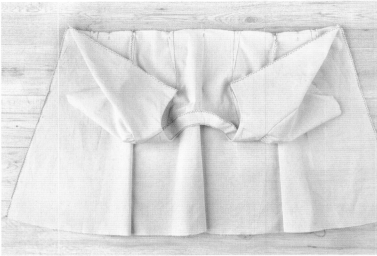

2 Pin the Skirt to the Bodice at the waistline (**RST**). Match the centre backs, then match each seam and dart before pinning in between. Getting your key points pinned helps to make an accurate garment. When you sew the seam, keep your pins in right until the stitch before each one, so the seams do not move. Neaten the seam allowances together.

3 Pin and sew up the centre-back seam to the bottom of where the zip will start.

4 Insert the zip (see pages 146–153).

5 Hem the sleeves and skirt section. There are two ways to hem:

a. Neaten the edge of the hem, press it up by 1cm (⅜in) and then stitch in place from the front. You will see the zigzag finish on the inside.

b. Press up the hem by 1cm (⅜in). You can choose to stitch the first fold in place, or just pin it in place. Press up again by 1cm (⅜in) and stitch in place from the front.

5a

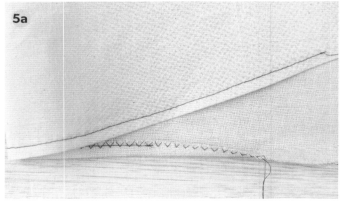

5b

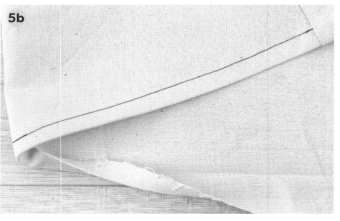

If your dress has a side-seam opening…

Follow steps 1 to 5 for the bodice and sleeves (pages 142–143).

1 On the bodice, pin and sew the centre-back seam. Neaten the seam allowances together.

2 On the side seam without a zip opening (usually the right side), pin and sew up your side seam. Neaten together.

3 On the side seam with the zip opening (usually the left side), pin and sew from the hem of the sleeve, to approximately 2cm (¾in) past the underarm seam. Leave the rest of the side seam open. Neaten the seam allowances separately.

4 On the skirt, pin and sew the centre-back seam. Neaten the seam allowances together.

5 Next, pin and sew the full length of the skirt's right side seam. Neaten the seam allowances together.

6 Then, on the skirt's left side seam, sew from the hem up to where the zip will start. Neaten the seam allowances separately.

7 Pin the skirt to the bodice at the waistline (**RST**), matching all the key features. Sew together. Neaten the waist seam allowances together.

8 Insert the zip (see pages 146–153).

9 Hem the sleeves and skirt section.

zip closures

As with everything in dressmaking, accurate preparation is key to a successful zip.

A lapped zip on a skirt.

A concealed zip on a skirt.

Zips are usually sewn in the centre-back seam, or side seam depending on where your opening is.

There are a few ways of inserting a zip, but I am going to focus on two methods that I think will be the most beneficial. The first method is a lapped zip and the second, which is my favourite, is the concealed zip.

The first few steps of both methods help you plan where to sew your seams together, and how to position the zip accurately.

Top tips for zips

- Choose the right length of zip. If the correct size is not available, always go longer than the opening, never shorter.
- Practise inserting zips first using scrap fabric, so you get the hang of it.
- Always tack (baste) a zip in place as fabrics and zips move when being sewn together!
- Avoid using zips with metal teeth as you will break a needle if you hit the metal.
- Nylon zips are perfect but make sure the teeth are not too bulky.
- Before sewing the zip in, make sure both seams are exactly the same length.

Positioning the zip

Zips always have extra tape at the top and bottom. Close your zip and you will see there is at least 1cm (⅜in) additional zip tape, sometimes more, above where the zip stops.

Whether you have a waistband finish or a facing finish, the method of positioning and inserting the zip is the same.

- Position the top of the zip pull a few millimetres below the finished waistband, or the seam of the facing, as shown right.

Waistband finish

Facing finish

Example of positioning a zip on a skirt from the right side of the fabric.

Tip

- If you are sewing a zip into a side-seam opening, position the zip pull just below the underarm seam so there is no gap.

LAPPED ZIP

A lapped zip is inserted so that one side of the seam laps over the teeth of the zip to hide it. This is the most common method for those new to dressmaking as it is simple. You don't need any special feet as most sewing machines come with a standard zipper foot.

Type of zip: Closed-end nylon zip

Type of foot: Standard zipper foot

Fabric used: Cotton

Seam allowance: 1.5cm (⅝in)

Neaten the seam allowances by either overlocking (serging) or with zigzag stitch. Try not to cut off much of your seam allowance if you use an overlocker (serger).

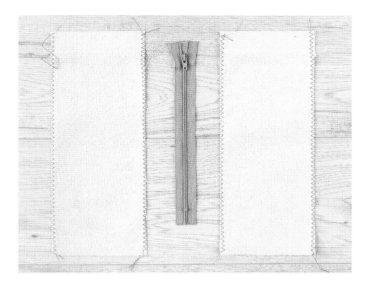

Preparing the seam

This is demonstrated below with a **waistband** finish.

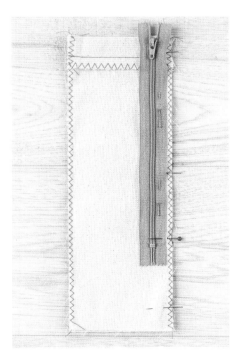

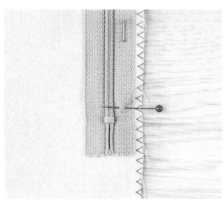

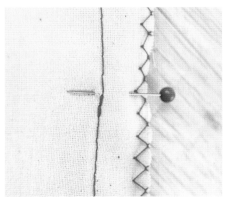

1 Place your seams right sides together (**RST**) with the finished edges in line. Line up any seams (waistband or waistline seams). Pin in place.

2 Position the zip on the seam edge, with the zip pull just below the top of the waistband. Pin in place.

3 Approximately 5mm (¼in) above the zip stopper (bottom), place a horizontal pin through the fabric. You do not want to sew through the stopper as you could snap your needle, so this is a key position.

4 Remove the zip but keep the pin in position.

5 Set your stitch length to the longest setting and sew a 1.5cm (⁹⁄₁₆in) seam allowance from the top of the waistband down to the pin. Stop at the pin. This is purely a tacking (basting) stitch so it needs to be easy to remove.

When at the pin, change your stitch length to 2.5 and do a backstitch to secure that spot. Continue sewing down the seam to the hem.

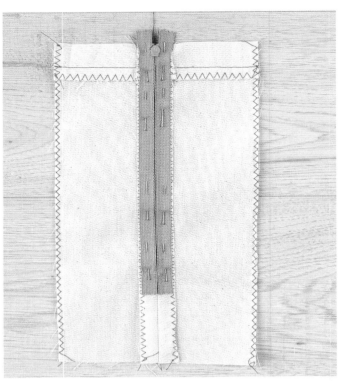

6 Press the seam open so that the seam allowances sit nice and flat.

7 Place your seam with the right sides facing down on the table and the seam allowances facing you. Place the zip face down, onto the seam. Position the zip pull just below the waistband, and the zip teeth in line with the centre of the seam.
Pin in place on both sides of the zip teeth.

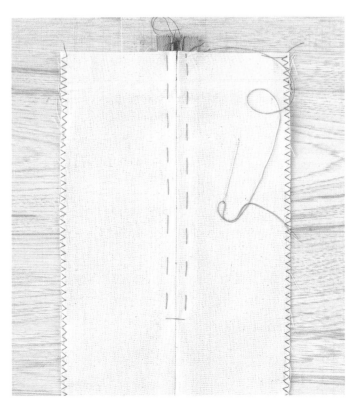

8 Feeling the teeth through the fabric, tack (baste) the zip in place using a contrasting colour. The tacking (basting) stitches should sit approximately 4mm (³⁄₁₆in) away from the teeth of the zip, so it isn't too snug. Remove the pins as you tack (baste).
You will always have a lumpy bit where the zip pull sits at the top, so tacking (basting) well will allow you to sew this as neatly as possible.

Tacking (basting) tip

• Try to keep your tacking (basting) stitch as neat as possible as you can use it as a guide for sewing. 1cm (³⁄₈in) long stitches and a 1cm (³⁄₈in) gap is usually a good guide.

Sewing the zip in place

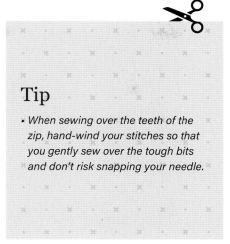

Tip

• *When sewing over the teeth of the zip, hand-wind your stitches so that you gently sew over the tough bits and don't risk snapping your needle.*

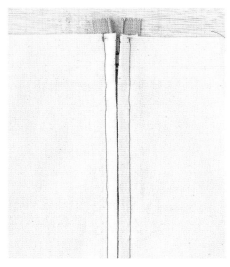

1 A zipper foot will allow you to sew close to the zip, on the right side of the fabric. Using your tacking (basting) as a guide, start at the top, sew down to just before the stopper, across and back up in a 'U' shape. Make sure to backstitch at the start and end.

   The zip pull will stay at the top, so you will need to go slowly and try not to wobble past it! It can be hard to get the stitching perfect, so use a matching thread colour to hide any wobbly bits.

2 Use a seam ripper to open up the machine-tacked/basted seam covering the teeth. Remove the hand-tacking (basting) as well.

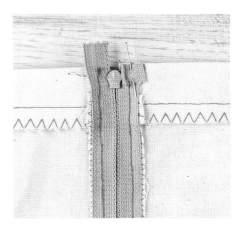

Waistband finish.

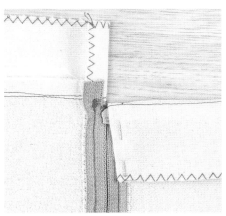

Facing finish.

3 On the inside, fold the excess zip tape back down onto itself and pin in place. For the facing, fold the excess zip tape and the facing to the back and pin in place. Hand-sew in position.

Right, two finished lapped zips.
It is impossible to hide the zip pull, so do your best to make it look neat.

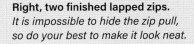

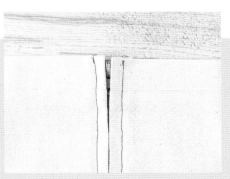

Waistband finish.

Facing finish.

CONCEALED ZIP

If you are feeling brave, why not try using a concealed zip for a super-neat finish? A concealed zip is the most discreet zip you can insert into clothing. It is a fiddly process when you first try it, but good preparation is key to a neat and accurate finish.

You will need to purchase a concealed zipper foot for your model of machine. I recommend asking a local sewing-machine shop to source one for you, so you get the right one. The difference with a concealed zip is the teeth are on the back of the zip, rather than the front. You see only the zip pull from the front.

Type of zip: Concealed nylon zip

Type of foot: Concealed zipper foot

Fabric used: Cotton

Seam allowance: 1cm (⅜in)

Neaten the seam allowances by either overlocking (serging) or with zigzag stitch. Try not to cut off much of your seam allowance if you use an overlocker (serger).

A concealed zip in place.

Preparing the seam

This is demonstrated below with a **waistband** finish.

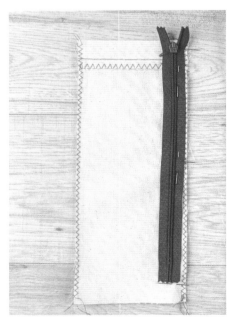

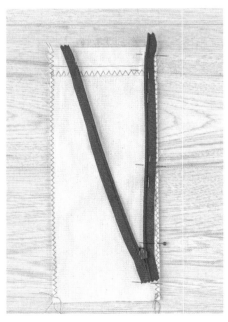

1 Place your seams right sides together (**RST**). Line up any seams (such as waistband or waistline seams). Pin in place.

2 Position the zip on the seam edge, with the zip pull just below the top of the waistband. Pin in place.

3 Undo the zip completely. Place a pin 5mm (¼in) above the top of the zip pull. This is a key position, so be accurate.

4 Remove the zip but keep the pin in position.

5 Sew the seam up to the exact position of the pin and backstitch well to secure in place. Press the stitched seam open but not the unsewn section.

6 Position the fabric with the right sides facing the table and the pressed seam allowances facing you. With the zip closed, place the concealed zip face down onto the seam opening.

As in step 2, position the zip with the zip pull just below the top of the waistband and raw edges together. Pin one side in place.

7 Then repeat on the other side of the zip, matching the zip position exactly at the top.

You are only pinning through the one layer of seam allowance. You should not see any pins from the front of the garment as no stitching should be visible on the outside.

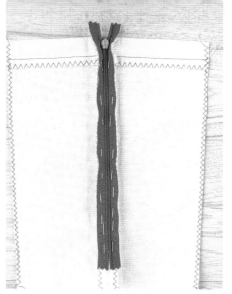

Back.   *Front.*

8 On one side, hand-tack (baste) the whole length of the zip in place using a contrasting thread. Remember, you are only sewing through the one layer of zip and one layer of fabric.

Keep your stitches about 7.5mm (⁵⁄₁₆in) apart and secure well at the top and bottom. Stitch approximately 3mm (⅛in) from the zip teeth.

9 On the remaining side, starting at the top, hand-tack (baste) down to about 1.5cm (⅝in) before the sewn seam. Do an extra hand-tack (baste) to keep it all in place at that point.

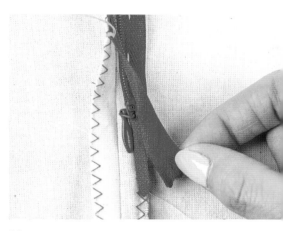

10 Unzip the zip. Lift the end of the zip and pull the zip pull through the gap to the back to unzip it fully. The zip should stop just below the top of the finished seam.

11 Pin the edge of the zip back onto the seam edge and continue to tack (baste) the last bit in place. Turn it over and check that everything is looking flat and neat from the right side.

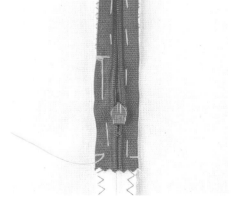

Wrong side.

Right side.

Sewing in the zip

1 Open the zip. Put your concealed zipper foot onto your machine and position the needle in the centre. You will sew on the wrong side of the zip. The teeth of the zip will be positioned in the grooves of the foot. The teeth will be rolled over slightly by the foot, so you can sew really close to them, making the zip invisible from the front.

2 Start 5mm (¼in) down from the top and backstitch to secure in place. Make sure the teeth of the zip are rolling away from your needle. You don't want to sew through the teeth, so gently help them into position at the start, if needed. The foot will keep the teeth rolled out, so you just need to sew the length of the zip. Keep everything flat when sewing. When you reach the zip pull and cannot sew any further, sew a backstitch to secure in place.

You should not see any stitching from the front of the garment.

3 Repeat on the other side of the zip, positioning the teeth in the other groove of the zipper foot.

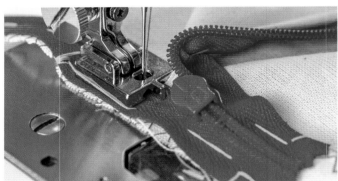

4 Take out the tacking (basting) at the bottom of the zip so that you can access the zip pull. Poke it through to the front so you can grab it and do the zip up. You should only be able to see the zipper pull as the zip should be concealed.

Hopefully, your seam is nice and flat and discreet. If so, you can then remove all of the tacking (basting) and do a little dance!

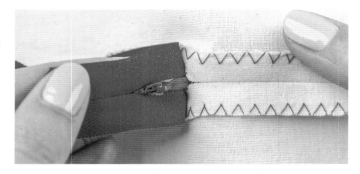

Poke your zip pull through the gap to the front.

Close your zip to check that it is sitting flat.

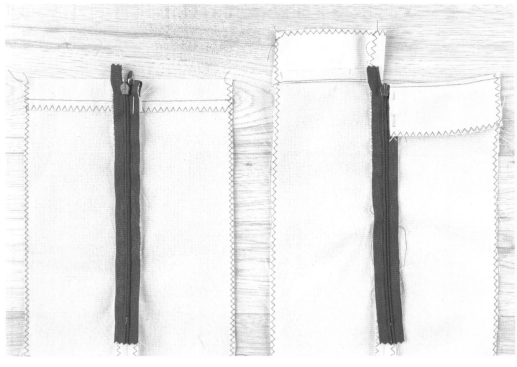

5 On the inside, for the waistband, fold the excess zip tape inbetween the seam allowance and the front. Pin in place. Hand-sew the zip to the seam allowance, then attach it to the top of the waistband.

If your skirt has a facing, fold the excess zip tape and the facing to the back and pin in place. Hand-sew to the zip.

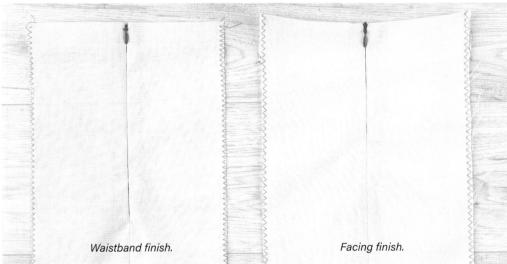

Waistband finish.

Facing finish.

Waistband and facing finishes from the right side.

6 My last tip is to sew the zip ends onto the seam allowance. I find this stops the zip pulling, especially if your zip is longer then your opening. Make sure you only sew on the seam allowance. You can hand-tack (baste) or do a quick machine stitch.

Concealed zips don't usually need ironing, but if you choose to, keep the iron on low and lightly use the tip of the iron on the seam itself.

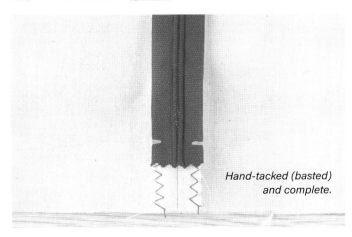

Hand-tacked (basted) and complete.

8 separates

With your altered patterns, you can create a simple, loose-fitting top. This can be paired with the skirts to create a really versatile wardrobe. You will need your Front Bodice and Back Bodice pattern pieces.

tops

FRONT BODICE

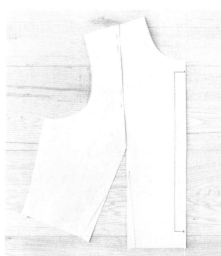

1 Trace around your Front Bodice pattern piece, without seam allowance. Cut it out.

2 Draw a line from the centre of the waist dart to meet the tip of the shoulder dart. It will look off centre but it is correct. Cut up the line and stop at the bust dart.

3 Close the shoulder dart and pin in place. This will flare out the bodice pattern and remove your shoulder dart. You won't have to sew this one now!

4 Trace around the newly flared bodice pattern.

5 Extend the length by 5–10cm (2–4in) so it sits below the waist. Gently curve the lower edge.

6 Extend your dart to meet the new hem, then draw a line down the centre of the new large dart.

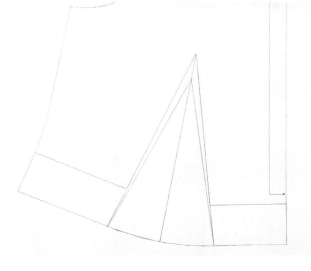

7 Move the tip of the dart down by approximately 3cm (1¼in) so that the tip is sitting below the bust point.

8 Re-draw your dart from the new tip – you can draw a narrower dart for a looser fit (as you will be taking out less fabric).

9 Mark armhole notches, grainline and 'cut 1 on the fold' on the centre front. Add 1cm (⅜in) seam allowances except on the centre front and the hem – the front is cut on the fold and the hem allowance will be added later.

BACK BODICE AND FINAL ADJUSTMENTS

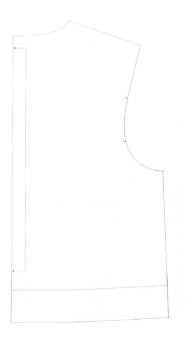

7 Close the front dart and pin in place. Fold the dart towards the side seam. Pin the side seams together and then re-draw the hem with a gentle curve. Make sure you have right angles on the centre-front and centre-back seams.

8 Add a seam allowance to the new hem and then cut off the excess.

9 Draw in your chosen neckline. Make sure you can get it over your head as you won't have a zip. Trace off facings for your neckline. Next, create patterns for your chosen sleeve or create facings for the armholes.

1 Now, trace around your Back Bodice pattern piece, without seam allowance.

2 The Back Bodice will be cut on the fold so make sure you mark 'cut on fold'.

3 For a looser fit, you won't sew the back darts so there is no need to mark them.

4 Extend the length the same amount as for the Front.

5 Mark armhole notches, grainline and 'cut 1 on the fold' on the centre back. Add 1cm (⅜in) seam allowances except on the centre back and the hem.

6 Cut around both pattern pieces but leave extra on the hem.

Cutting and sewing your top

1 Cut one Front Bodice, one Back Bodice and both front and back neck facings on the fold.

2 Sew the front waist darts.

3 Sew the shoulder seams on the top and also on the facings. Neaten the seams together and finish the facing edge.

4 Sew your facings to the neckline. Snip into the seam allowance and then understitch.

5 Sew facings onto your armholes or attach sleeves.

6 Sew the side seams and then neaten the seam allowances together.

7 Neaten the hem, turn up and sew in place. Press to finish.

skirts: adding a waistband or facing

When creating a skirt, you will need to add a waistband or a facing to finish the waist seam properly.

For the fitted styles, I would add a facing as it allows you to neaten the waistline seam and add a little bit of structure to the waist, all without the positioning of the waistline and hips changing.

A narrow waistband will sit better on the skirts that aren't fitted, as the waistband will sit comfortably on the waistline and the skirt will sit a little lower. You want to keep the waistband 2cm (¾in) wide or less.

If your fabric is fine or even floaty, you can interface the waistband to give it the structure it needs. (See page 100.)

PATTERN CUTTING YOUR WAISTBAND

1 Measure the full waistline on the finished pattern pieces, with no seam allowances.

2 Draw a horizontal line across a piece of paper half the length of your waistline. Square down at both ends.

3 Draw a parallel line 1cm (⅜in) below. (Seam allowance.)

4 Draw a parallel line 2cm (¾in) below. (Front of waistband.)

5 Draw a parallel line 2cm (¾in) below. (Back of waistband.)

6 Draw a parallel line 1cm (⅜in) below. (Seam allowance.)

7 Label one end of the line (shown on the right) as 'centre' and write 'cut × 1 on fold.'

8 Using your front pattern piece, measure the distance from the centre seam to the side seam. Mark this on your waistband as a notch.

9 Add a seam allowance to the centre-back seam (which is the left-hand end of the waistband pattern shown above).

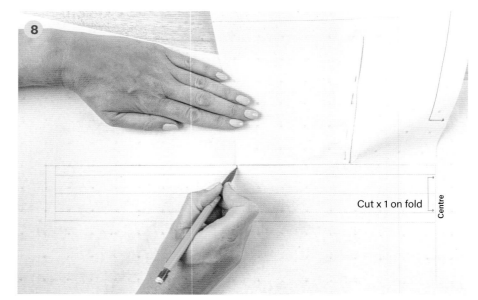

Cut x 1 on fold   Centre

10 Cut the waistband out on the fold.

11 Fold the waistband in half lengthways and try it on your waist. Sometimes, a snug fit works better on a skirt so you can cut 1cm (⅜in) off the centre-back seams of your skirt and waistband, for a better fit.

ATTACHING YOUR WAISTBAND

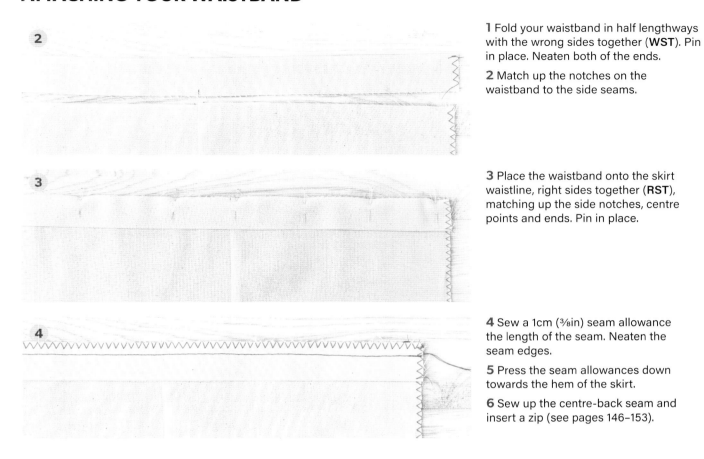

1 Fold your waistband in half lengthways with the wrong sides together (**WST**). Pin in place. Neaten both of the ends.

2 Match up the notches on the waistband to the side seams.

3 Place the waistband onto the skirt waistline, right sides together (**RST**), matching up the side notches, centre points and ends. Pin in place.

4 Sew a 1cm (⅜in) seam allowance the length of the seam. Neaten the seam edges.

5 Press the seam allowances down towards the hem of the skirt.

6 Sew up the centre-back seam and insert a zip (see pages 146–153).

The sewn waistband.

PATTERN CUTTING YOUR FACING

Refer to pages 98–99 for instructions on how to draft a neck facing. Use the same process for your skirt facing, as described here.

1 If you have darts on the skirt pattern pieces, pin them closed.

2 Trace off 6cm- (2⅜in-) deep facings for your Back Skirt and Front Skirt patterns.

3 Label your facings with notches, side seams and centres.

SEWING ON YOUR FACING

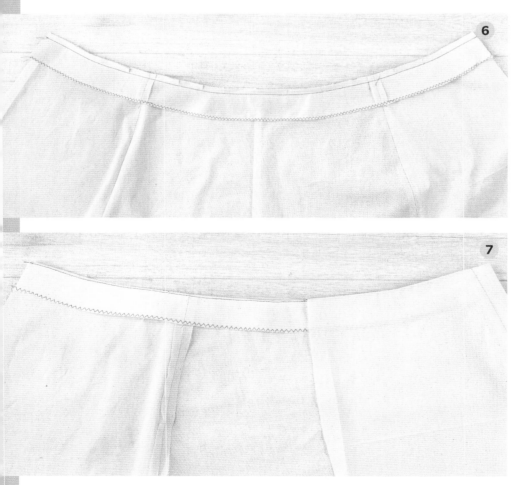

1 Block fuse the wrong side of the fabric before cutting out your facings (see page 100).

2 Pin and sew the side seams of the skirt together. Neaten the seam allowances together.

3 Sew the side seams of the facings together. Press seams open.

4 Sew the facings to the skirt at the waistline, right sides together.

5 Neaten the long raw edge of the facing.

6 Snip into any curves in the waistline seam allowance.

7 Understitch (see page 102).

8 Pin and sew up the centre-back seam to the zip opening.

9 Neaten the seam allowances open.

10 Insert the zip (see page 146).

11 Hem the skirt (page 144).

9 taking it further

When you have perfected your fit and you have your unique set of dress patterns finished, you could consider taking your ideas further. Try different fabric combinations for each dress that you make as they will be transformed in look and shape. Little decorative additions can also have a big impact. Consider some of the following:

Patch pockets   Patch pockets in contrasting fabrics would be a welcome addition to the straight or A-line skirts. Simply cut out your desired shape, fold in the seam allowances and stitch onto your dress.

Buttons   Buttons are a brilliant way to make an outfit totally unique. You can either use buttons decoratively on a collar, or keep them functional.

Piping   Piping could be used in the seams of the straight or A-line skirt. It could also be used in the outer seam of the collar for a highly decorative look.

Collars   You can play with different shapes and sizes of collars to drastically change the look of a dress. Have fun with it!

Embroidery   Embroidery can be a really enjoyable way of making a dress/garment totally unique. You can reinforce the areas you plan to stitch by ironing a layer of interfacing onto the back.

I look forward to seeing where this dressmaking journey takes you next!

index

advanced pattern alterations   86–90
  full-bust alteration (FBA)   89–90
  gaping armhole   86
  rounded back   88
  allowing for a zip opening   80
alterating   10, 40, 45, 52, 55, 58, 74–80, 83, 86,
  adding onto the hips   46, 55, 57
  adding onto the waist   46, 56
  taking off the bodice side seams   46, 57
  waist and hips   55–57
arranging patterns on fabric

block fusing   10, 99, 100
block(s)   8, 32–34, 42, 44, 46, 48, 50–51, 52–59, 74,
  77, 82, 93, 99, 104, 108, 117, 122, 123, 129
  choosing the right size   44
bust   12, 33, 37, 41–46, 50–52, 55, 56–57, 61, 67, 68,
  75, 76, 86–87, 89–90, 123, 154, 155

calico   8, 25, 28, 60, 63, 84, 90
circle(s)
  mathematical method   116–117, 128–129
  traditional method   116–117, 128–129
collars   8–9, 43, 136–138, 159

dart(s)   33, 37, 49, 52–55, 57, 58–59, 62, 64–70, 78,
  80, 84–90, 93, 96, 97, 98, 100, 122–123, 125, 128, 130,
  132, 135, 136, 142, 144, 154–155, 158
  continual dart 'cheat technique'   68
  double-pointed   67
dress, fitted   44, 125

fabric(s)   10, 12, 16–17, 18–22, 24–31, 32, 34, 35, 37,
  39, 43, 44, 47, 52, 60–68, 76, 80, 86, 90, 92, 98–100,
  104–106, 108, 112, 116, 119, 122, 126, 127, 128, 129, 130,
  132, 136–137, 146–151, 158–149,
facing(s)   10, 38, 94, 95, 96, 97, 98–103, 105, 122, 125,
  127, 131, 135, 137, 138, 142–143, 146, 148, 149, 153, 155,
  156–158
  for necklines   98–103
fastening(s)   22, 38, 93
fastening(s)
  zip(s), zip closure(s)   0, 12, 22, 36, 38, 70–72, 80,
  122, 124–125, 127, 129, 131, 134, 141, 142, 144, 145,
  146–153, 155, 157, 158
    concealed   12, 38, 80, 146, 150–153
    lapped   38, 146, 147–149

graded nest of patterns   33, 48
grainline(s)   10, 33, 34–35, 49, 50, 51, 56, 61, 99, 108,
  109, 110–111, 113, 116, 130, 132, 55
  understanding the grain   34–35

interfacing   10, 98, 100, 137, 159

key measurements   41–43, 44–45
  sizing tips   41

layplan   26, 60

neckline(s)   8–9, 10, 12, 22, 27, 34, 38, 43, 47, 50, 52,
  53, 63, 64, 72, 76, 78, 80, 85, 87, 90, 92–103
notch(es)   33, 36, 49, 50, 59, 62, 64, 65, 70, 71, 72, 82,
  83, 94–101, 104, 105, 106, 108, 109, 111–114, 116, 123, 124,
  126, 130, 132, 133, 139, 140, 155, 156, 158

overlocker (serger)   12, 17, 22, 100, 147, 150

paper pattern   8, 10, 59, 62, 64, 74, 77–80, 132, 136,
pattern
  cutting   31, 34, 48–51, 139, 156, 158
  markings   10, 12, 34
    adding   59
  master   10, 36, 58, 93
  paper   10, 53, 63, 94, 95, 96, 97, 109, 111, 113, 116, 118,
  piece(s)   8, 25, 32–33, 34–37, 42, 48–51, 52–53,
    58–59, 60–64, 67, 76, 78–80, 82–83, 88–89, 93,
    97–100, 109–111, 113–114, 116, 119, 122–124, 126, 128,
    130–132, 136, 139, 154–155, 156, 158
      cutting out   59
  pinning [...] in place   62
  preparing to trace   48
  tracing off   8, 33, 46, 48, 49–51, 52, 55, 74, 77,
    82–83, 86, 90, 93, 98, 108, 110, 113, 116, 123, 130, 132,
    136, 139, 155, 158
piping   159
pleat(s)   9, 22, 27, 30, 37, 39, 87, 122, 132–134, 142
pocket(s)   8–9, 139–141

sample (toile)   8, 25, 28, 44, 46, 48, 52, 60–90, 92,
  103, 142
  centre-back opening   71, 76
  pinning and sewing   69–72
  side-seam opening   72, 76, 145, 146
seam(s)   12, 18, 20–22, 25, 26, 29, 36–37, 46, 50,
  52–59, 60, 66, 69, 70, 71, 72, 74–80, 82–83, 84–85,
  86–89, 93, 94, 95, 96, 97, 98–102, 105–107, 111, 112,
  114–115, 116–119, 122–125, 126–127, 128–129, 130–131,
  132–133, 134, 137, 138, 139, 140–141, 142–145, 146–149,
  150–153, 155, 156–158, 159
  neatening   22
    sewing zigzag stitch   12, 15, 22, 100, 144,
      147, 150
  pressing   21

seam allowance   10, 12, 18–20, 22, 36, 48, 58–59, 60,
  62, 64, 69, 70, 74, 78–80, 82–83, 86–90, 93, 94, 95,
  96, 97, 98, 100–103, 105, 108–109, 110–111, 112, 113–115,
  116–117, 119, 123–127, 128–129, 130–131, 132–134,
  136–137, 139–140, 147, 150–151, 153, 154–158
sewing machine   10, 12, 14–17, 19, 20, 22, 29, 102, 127,
  147, 150
  needle(s)   16–17, 18–19, 20–22, 29, 30, 31, 104, 146,
    147, 149, 152
  thread tension   17
size chart   8, 32, 44–46
sizing in practice   46
skirt(s)   8–9, 12, 22, 27, 32, 37, 38, 39, 43, 44, 47, 48,
  51, 55–58, 60–61, 64, 69, 70, 72, 76, 77, 80, 84, 85, 87,
  90, 92, 120, 121, 122–135, 139–141, 142, 144–145, 146,
  153, 154, 156–158, 159
  altering the length   58
slash and spread   108, 116–117, 128
sleeve(s)   8–9, 12, 22, 27, 32, 34, 37, 39, 42, 43, 47, 48,
  69, 72, 76, 80, 83–83, 86, 87, 90, 92, 103, 104–119, 120,
  121, 125, 127, 135, 142–145, 155
  choosing the correct size   82–83
    bicep alteration   83
sleeveless dress   76, 103
stretch fabrics   24, 31

thread(s)   10, 17, 20–22, 29, 65, 66, 104–106, 114–115,
  127, 149, 151
toile, see: sample
transferring your alterations to the
  paper pattern   77–80
  transferring your new marks   77–80

understitching   102–103, 140
useful extra measurements   42–43

waistband   39, 72, 120, 122, 125, 127, 129, 131, 134,
  146–150, 153, 156–157,
waistline   50, 53–55, 64, 67–70, 76–80, 85, 122–123,
  126–127, 128–129, 132–133, 134, 139, 144–145, 147, 150,
  156–158
wearing ease   44–46, 86